Freestyle

ANDY FROST works as an evangelist for Share Jesus International, a mission agency whose goal is summed up by its name – to share Jesus in many different contexts and countries. He is involved in pioneering new styles of mission, in particular with surf, skate and club culture. He has preached all over the country in a variety of contexts ranging from university Christian Union weekends to skate competitions, night clubs and national conferences. Andy loves to surf and is learning how to breakdance. A regular writer for *thewalk* magazine, he has also co-written a cross-generational book with his family, *Destiny* (published by Authentic). He is involved in local youth work, is part of the Billy Graham Evangelism Institute and is training to be a local preacher. Andy is part of the leadership team of Café Church and leads a football team.

JO WELLS is a natural relational evangelist with a passion for seeing the church better equipped to both disciple and mentor young and new Christians. Jo has spoken at Easter People, SOULINTHECITY and led the Destiny Leadership programme. Working full time for Share Jesus International, she is responsible for the pastoral support of the youth network, and works with Andy in the mission and discipleship initiatives throughout the year. She is also involved in the local school and youth work in south-west London and is training as a local preacher. Jo is also a leader at Café Church and is part of the Billy Graham Evangelism Institute.

Freestyle

Living the extreme life

ANDY FROST and JO WELLS

11   10   09   08   07   06   05   7   6   5   4   3   2   1

First published 2005 by Authentic Media,
9 Holdom Avenue, Bletchley, Milton Keynes MK1 1QR, UK
and 129 Mobilization Drive, Waynesboro, GA 30830–4575, USA

www.authenticmedia.co.uk

British Library Cataloguing in Publication Data

A catalogue record for this book is available from the British Library

ISBN 1–85078–619–4

Cover Design by Sam Redwood
Typeset by Waverley Typesetters, Galashiels
Print Management by Adare Carwin
Printed and Bound by J. H. Haynes & Co. Ltd., Sparkford

*Dedicated to all those that have encouraged us
to live the extreme life ...*

*Special cheers to Sarah Philips and for the poetic genius of
Marcy Burnham and 29th Chapter's MC McGladius.*

*Thanks Jesus for the journey so far –
may we keep living for you ...*

Contents

trapped in materialism

threatened by apathy

disillusioned with postmodernity

lost in conformity

searching for reality

desperate for more

the cry is for *freedom*

foreword

gavin calver

As I sat there listening to the evangelist on the stage I was totally captivated by his every word. Even though I was lost amidst a sea of teenagers, it felt like he was speaking directly to me. He spoke of his experiences as a Christian in a way that brought his story to life amazingly. By the time that he had finished, I knew that I had no choice but to respond. I realized that Jesus had died for me, loved me, knew everything about me and was desperate for me to follow Him. As a young man of fifteen, I decided to become a Christian.

As the speaker finished, I got up to my feet and joined many young people who were going forward to become Christians. Just before making my final move to the front, doubts swept into my mind: What about those people in church – I'll have to be like them? What about all those rules I'll have to follow? How can I ever hope to be a good Christian, it's just too hard? I agreed with all that the speaker was saying but I didn't want to be a Christian if it meant being like all the ones I'd experienced. Suddenly my desperate desire to follow this Jesus that the evangelist described so vividly, was counteracted by my fear of becoming religious. I had to make a decision, so instead of going forward and surrendering my life to Jesus I chose to sit back down again and keep living for myself.

It wasn't until a few years later that I finally became a Christian. I knew Jesus existed but it all seemed too much and so boring. As a teenager, it seemed impossible to live the whole thing out. What with my body changing rapidly, many exams to pass, girls to go out with and fun to be had, becoming a Christian appeared to be a thankless task, with little or no chance of realistic success.

In this wonderful book, Andy and Jo have put things in a perspective that would have helped me immensely when I was younger. They bring to life this radical revolutionary called Jesus who, through walking on earth, changed the course of history forever. They give hope to every young person that Christianity is a real option to them, often in spite of the church. Through their strong personal stories, they show us what it means to be part of the Kingdom of God. It's not about sitting in a stuffy old building singing stuffy old songs but, instead, about following the most amazing of all Kings.

However, it would be a mistake to assume that this book is just full of inspiration and excitement, when there is so much more to it than that. With a charismatic personality it only takes a moment to get excited, yet far more than just excitement is needed to act upon these words. Throughout this book, Andy and Jo provide many helpful tips and suggestions in order to make one's faith a lifestyle. All of the major aspects of the Christian faith are covered, from the importance of Scripture to the power of prayer, the necessity of worship to the importance of social justice. Each page echoes the fullness of what it means to be a radical disciple without compromise.

Thankfully, and bravely, they even mention the thing that makes many Christians shudder: the unquestionable need to share our own faith without giving way to fear. When they speak of adopting a 'scare myself' attitude to evangelism the challenge is immense. After all, it's so easy to share Jesus in the safe place, but the real challenge comes in living and sharing Him with all types of people, whether you feel able to or not. This attitude, coupled with the practical suggestions for authentic living sum up the essence of this book – what it means to be a history maker. Gone are the days when young people can sit back and leave it to the adults. We must follow this radical Jesus who, after making his mark on history, commands that we, his disciples, do the same. This man who gave life to the dead, bread to the hungry, integrity to the sinner and acceptance to the marginalized, requires us to mirror this in our lives today.

Andy and Jo don't just hide away in a Christian bubble and write this stuff. You'll discover that they know what it is to be out of their comfort zone, how it feels to follow Jesus with everything and what it means to depend on Him when all else fails. That's what makes this book so powerful. They earn the right to write what they have because they walk the walk. This book gives you, the reader, a choice: you can continue living your life your way or you can actually make a real difference to your world right now! Don't wait until you're older to start – live it today. You don't start making history when you leave school – you start now!

I am personally so pleased that *Freestyle* has been written. If I'd had access to this book when I was 15, my response to the evangelist may well have been different. I plead with you to do one thing as you begin to read the pages beyond: finish this book, look at your life and ask the Lord what needs to change. If you live in line with what is said here, then you won't go too far wrong. I'm overjoyed that they have written this tremendous book, let's go and write history together!

GAVIN CALVER
Director of Church Resource, Youth for Christ
December 2004

Jesus revolutionary

andy frost and jo wells

I looked down from the bridge that crossed the ravine between the two cliff tops. Tiny paddle-boats slowly manoeuvred their way along the crystal clear waterway in what looked like the ideal setting for a mineral water ad. The bridge was a busy two-lane road of traffic and there were a number of tourists scattered along its high railing, admiring the view. Holding tightly to the top, I climbed over the metal railing and decided that I was going to do it.

As I prepared for the biggest jump of my life into the river below, my mind was suddenly invaded by two voices. They argued away in my head. The first voice is the adventurous one urging you on to make the jump. It dares you, challenging your adventurous spirit. This voice reminds you of the glory, if you make it ...

Then there is the other voice – the one that sounds like a sensible parent telling you not to be stupid. This voice highlights the dangers and the fears. I looked down at the lake below. By this time other people on the bridge had seen that I had crossed over the barrier and began to gather around pointing at me – me, this brave young boy. Some people even started taking photographs. Was this to be the last photo of Andy Frost before he plunged to his death?

The pressure was mounting and as the crowd grew all around me, the embarrassment factor grew. I knew that I couldn't merely cross over the barrier back to the safety of the pavement. I drew a deep breath and leapt into the air.

I had been jumping all that day. Normally it took a split second before the cool water rushed over my body. But this was different. I was falling but I just didn't seem to be hitting the water. I looked down and all I could see was my feet pointing straight towards the water that was hurtling towards me. I could hear the sound of the air rushing past my ears and I decided to stop focusing on the river and keep my head up.

Finally, I felt the water as my feet crashed through its surface with the rest of me following. I went deep and pain seared through my body as I came back up to the surface. My ears rang and I felt totally disorientated. My back hurt and the severe winding, like a punch to the stomach, meant that all I could do was groan. I tried to swim to the side, aware that the crowd would still be watching as they peered over the rail, tens of metres above, but my body was having none of it – all I could manage was a pathetic doggy paddle!

The Choice

Every day we are faced with choices. We choose what to wear, we choose what to eat, we choose what to watch and we choose what to read. All of these choices flow from who we are and most importantly, what or who we choose to follow. Irvine Walsh looked at the issue of choice in the cult film classic, *Trainspotting*. The monologue below lists some of our options. As Christians we have chosen to turn our back on things of this world. We choose to follow Jesus instead. Both Jo and I have made this choice …

What's the point?

I love adventure. I love doing crazy and extreme things. From a young age I have never wanted to live a boring life and I used to think that being a Christian meant being boring. I didn't want to choose that.

'What's the point in becoming a Christian now? I want to go out and live life. I want to get drunk, sleep around, and do fun stuff ... then, when I am about 80, just before I die, I will say a prayer and I can still get to heaven.'

What a cool life plan I used to think. I had it sorted! I thought I was so clever. Odds are, I will probably live to a ripe old age. I can then make that choice to accept God's forgiveness on my deathbed. Why waste life in church meetings when I could get the best of both worlds – literally.

However, what I had not understood was that being a Christian was not just about heaven. Heaven is of course a big slice of the action but it is not the whole thing. Being a Christian is not about sitting in church waiting to die. Being a Christian is in fact about having a relationship with the Living God now! It's about knowing the God that created the world! Being a Christian is about following Jesus. At the age of 18, I made the choice to follow this Jesus, not some character in a fairy tale, but the most radical guy that ever lived.

Andy Frost

Choose life. Choose a job. Choose a career. Choose a family. Choose a ... big television, choose washing machines, cars, compact disc players and electrical tin-openers ... Choose good health, low cholesterol and dental insurance. Choose fixed-interest mortgage repayments. Choose a starter home. Choose your friends ... Choose DIY and wondering who ... you are on Sunday morning. Choose sitting on that couch watching mind-numbing, spirit-crushing game shows, stuffing ... junk food into your mouth. Choose rotting away at the end of it all ... nothing more than an embarrassment to the selfish ... brats you spawned to replace yourself. Choose your future. Choose life. but why would I want to do a thing like that? I chose not to choose life: I chose something else.

Trainspotting, 1996

What's the problem?

I always thought I was a Christian. 'Confess Jesus as Lord, know that he died on the cross for your sins and you're a Christian.' That's what I had been told and that is what I had understood. Being a Christian was about saying a prayer and going to church.

Tick! Done that! Nice one! And I just carried on living. My life did not change. I had said my prayer and that was all I thought I needed to do. I continued getting drunk and sleeping around – what was the problem?

Then came a point in my life when I suddenly began to grasp what it meant to be a Christian. It meant more than saying a prayer – it meant putting my faith in God and following Jesus. Choosing to be a Christian meant choosing God's agenda and allowing His Spirit to change me.

I had been living my life, according to my own rules, not according to God's. Aged 19, I committed my life to God and began to trust that God's ways were better than mine. Now things were different – I was on a journey with God. God had control over my life, and life finally made sense.

Jo Wells

The radical Jesus

Being a Christian is not about waiting to die. Being a Christian is not just about saying a prayer and attending church. Being a Christian is about going on an adventure with Jesus. When you jump into a relationship with Him, the ride begins – following the most radical man that ever lived.

He was so radical that He walked up to a blind guy, spat on the floor and put a cocktail of mud and spit into the blind geezer's eyes – totally healing him.

He was so radical that He walked up to a coffin surrounded by mourners and told the little dead boy in the coffin to get up.

He was so radical that He defended the prostitute and loved the outcast.

He was so radical that when He was arrested, He did not plead for His life but kept silent.

He was so radical that He didn't just die but He rose to life again.

He was so radical that He didn't only speak of a new kingdom but He revealed it with His actions.

And then He offers me and you the chance to know Him – more than that, He offers us a chance to be adopted into His family and to have 'life – life in all it's fullness' (Jn. 10:10). He offers us every spiritual blessing right here right now (Eph. 1:3) and a chance to be a revolutionary, changing the world. We have discovered that following Jesus is not about living a half-full life of boredom – substituting excitement with mundane religiosity – it's about following the radical Jesus and being radical people. The adventure is long and hard and the choice to follow is yours.

Freestyle?

God is calling us into a new understanding of freedom (Gal. 5). God is calling each of us into a unique relationship with Him to explore our identity. God is calling us to express who we are in Him in the world around us. God is calling us for such a time as this.

> A Christian is someone whose life demands a spiritual explanation.
>
> Stephen Oldfield,
> sermon given in Edinburgh, 1986

Our desire has to be for more of Jesus – for Him to increase and for us to decrease (Jn. 3:30). This means taking more responsibility for our walk with God rather than relying on weekly pre-packaged sermons. This means doing not just what we have been told but understanding the reasoning behind it. This means digging deeper in our relationship with God – spending time chatting and listening to Him. And we hope that *Freestyle* will be a tool to help you keep focused. Go for it freestyle – living in God's freedom and in relationship with Him. Are you up for it?

Learn the script, follow the rule book and read the instruction manual
Better perform well in front of the Pop Idol panel
Same old tricks, techniques and tactics
Amateur dramatics, verbal gymnastics and 'get by' charismatics
Sleepless in Seattle, now you're up a creek without a paddle
You cannot expect to master, if you're only prepared to dabble
Followed the rabble, surfed too many music channels
Listened to the voices, now your minds trapped in the tower of Babble
Programmed, packaged and ready for purchase
Tell someone your story and I am sure they'll say … 'I've heard this'
But this feels allergic cause it stirred up reaction
Like asthma, you need an inhaler
Embracing what is weak is simply strange behaviour
The dynamics are not mathematical. Pie is not defined
The fence has loads of place mats; there is no shame in walking blind.

K. G. McGlade

1

the call and the cost

andy frost

As I looked out of the aeroplane window at the island of Mauritius sat in the Indian Ocean bathing in the sun, I was full of excitement – good waves, beautiful beaches and some mission thrown in! The fortnight started so well but a couple of days into the trip and this honeymoon paradise was under threat from a massive cyclone that was headed directly for us. Like a time-bomb waiting to explode, we found ourselves securing the rented accommodation, bringing in plant pots and fixing towels to stop water seeping through the windows – waiting for the storm to arrive.

We watched out of the French maisonette windows as the grey clouds on the horizon headed straight towards us. As time passed, the trees became more animated as the wind howled through the street and the rain poured like a waterfall. As the storm began to worsen, the power went out and our mission team sat watching a live cyclone trash the garden.

The cyclone was due to last almost two days. As boredom began to hit, we imagined what it would be like to struggle against the elements outside in the cyclone. Eventually, the excitement had over-whelmed us and common sense was switched off for an opportunity to play in the cyclone. Wearing only our boardies, we lined up by the front door and prepared for mayhem. As soon as the door was opened it was as if there was a full gale blowing inside the house. We pushed against the wind and found ourselves pinned against the wall surrounded by deafening howls and pleating rain. We stood tussling to keep to our feet. Some of the group decided that it was best to stay put with the wall as back-up.

A few of us were not content with standing by the wall and decided to battle against the wind to the end of the garden. Our goal was to reach a solitary tree being battered by the wind. It was as if everything was in slow motion as we struggled to walk against the blasts of wind. Each step was so dramatic and took for ever. Every part of my body was working together to keep motoring towards the goal – my eyes firmly fixed on the tree. Finally, we reached the edge of the garden and my arms embraced the tree, desperate for something sturdy to hold on to.

Andy Frost

Being a Jesus revolutionary is not about standing against the wall, cowering in safety. As Christians we are called to push into new frontiers, taking new ground, battling against the elements. Being a disciple of Christ is no easy ticket. Christianity is no crutch to lean on but a call to be counter-cultural. It is the most demanding thing that you can do with your life. There are many promises throughout the Bible of God's goodness but there are also many promises of difficult times. We are told that '... everyone who wants to live a godly life in Christ Jesus will be persecuted' (2 Tim. 3:12). Jesus calls us to pick up our cross and follow Him. The call of the church is to press on towards the goal that has been set before us – bringing

God's kingdom here on earth. The cost is to surrender our lives to Him, so that He can transform us.

The wake-up call

The call is not for lone mavericks but for Jesus revolutionaries to work together as a community to further His kingdom. The church is the most amazing movement in history. Starting with a group of radicals in Jerusalem, the movement has spread into almost every country on earth. And we are a part of it!

In the Bible, the church is described as the bride of Christ (Rev. 21:2). But in the Western world, when we look at the church we do not see a beautiful pure bride in a white dress transfixed with love for Jesus. The church's potential is lost in her sleepy relationship with God. Like the little girl that Jesus wakes up, we need God to reawaken the church for the church is not dead but merely sleeping (Mk. 5:21–43).

The big compromise

When I was 18 I went to work for a summer on a Salvation Army children's camp. Each week a new batch of children would come in and we would take them to do a variety of activities including canoeing, rock-climbing and camping. Then there came a week which catered for young people, many of whom were given a place on the camp for free. I remember meeting my cabin's young people. There were seven of them and they were scary. A couple of them had tattoos down their arms from the gangs with which they were associated.

'The good news is no longer good news, it is okay news. Christianity is no longer life-changing, it is life-enhancing. Jesus doesn't change people into wide-eyed radicals any more, he changes them into "nice people".

If Christianity is simply about being nice, I'm not interested. What happened to radical Christianity, the un-nice brand of Christianity that turned the world upside down? What happened to the category-smashing, life-threatening, anti-institutional gospel that spread through the first century like wildfire and was considered (by those in power) dangerous? What happened to the kind of Christians whose hearts were on fire, who had no fear, who spoke the truth no matter what the consequence, who made the world uncomfortable, who were willing to follow Jesus wherever he went? What happened to the kind of Christians who were filled with passion and gratitude and whom every day were unable to get over the Grace of God? I'm ready for a Christianity that "ruins" my life, that captures my heart and makes me uncomfortable. I want to be filled with an astonishment which is so captivating that I am considered wild and unpredictable and ... well ... dangerous. Yes, I want to be "dangerous" to a dull and boring religion. I want a faith that is considered "dangerous" by our predictable and monotonous culture.'

Robert Farrar Capon, *The Astonished Heart*
(Eerdmans Publishing Co, 1996)

Over the week they stayed, I had the opportunity to tell them about Jesus. During the week in which I worked with them I asked if they were up for becoming Jesus followers and knowing God. We prayed and they felt

God's Spirit. Blown away by the experience and having prayed for forgiveness and a new start, I then told them that they were now Christians. When they heard that they had become Christians, they were really confused. They were up for this following Jesus stuff but they reckoned that becoming Christians meant becoming boring. They understood Christianity as a series of rules that stopped people from having fun. How is it, that Christianity has got such a bad name?

Many people's perceptions of Christianity emerge from their experiences in church meetings. I can remember that in my teen years I was excited about the stuff that happened in the Bible but couldn't get my head around the fact that church seemed so different. Some churches were about people singing stuffy hymns and listening to an old person talk in monotone, others were about singing happy songs, clapping and patting themselves on the back – they seemed to have nothing in common with the rescue mission of the Bible. Surely church wasn't meant to be so inward focused?

In the book of Acts, the church is full of action – people were joining the disciples every day and they were seeing awesome stuff happen. At the same time they were being persecuted. The message that they preached was controversial and the establishment didn't like it. They spoke of Jesus as being their Lord, not the Roman emperor. What exciting times! But how did the church get from being this cutting-edge body of revolutionary people to what it looks like today?

I believe that much of the problem can be summed up in one word – *compromise*. Throughout time Christians have compromised the gospel. The gospel is the most radical message ever – God allowed His Son to die in your place and in mine. It turns the world upside down. It is a message that calls for repentance and transformation.

It is a message that blows away our understanding of the world and allows us to see another dimension. It is a message that has more martyrs than any other cause. It is the message that divides history between 'before Christ' and 'after'. But it is a message that Christians continue to water down with the things of this world. Time and time again, people become complacent about their relationship with God and content with the state of the world. They sacrifice relationship for stale religion – the ultimate compromise.

People have been complacent in their relationship with God since the beginning of time. People have chosen the created over the Creator. It all started with Adam who chose the apple and knowledge over his relationship with God. Imagine being in the Garden of Eden walking and talking with God. Yet Adam and Eve chose to do what they thought was best rather than trusting in God. They chose to jeopardize a relationship with the living God for things of this world. The pattern has continued throughout history. The Old Testament captures a recurring cycle. God sends His blessing on His people. God's people become complacent, enjoying the blessing but forgetting God. They turn their backs on Him and God has to call someone to bring them back into relationship with Him. We see this really clearly in the book of Judges and the books of the prophets.

Finally, God sent Jesus, His Son, to be the way, the truth and the life (Jn. 14:6). But even after the amazing miracle of Jesus' death and glorious resurrection, the church has been going through times of complacency and decay, interspersed with seasons of re-birth and revival. We read in the New Testament letters about compromise in the church, and then John in Revelation speaks of the church of Laodicea being lukewarm – neither hot nor cold. How quickly the message is compromised!

The story continues across the centuries. Throughout time people have tried to make following Jesus a life based on keeping laws and joining institutions – turning the church into a lukewarm establishment rather than a powerful movement. In the eighteenth century the Church of England had become very stale – run by the rich gentry rather than those passionate for Jesus. God called John Wesley to shake it up. Though he was an Anglican vicar, he was frequently banned from preaching from the lectern and preached instead from tombstones in graveyards, on hillsides or even on his horse! He preached Jesus and saw the church become a movement once again.

It is time for a new generation of men and women to wake up. I believe that God is calling revolutionaries to bring the church out of religiosity. I believe He is calling people to start putting Jesus at the centre. I believe He is calling people to start taking the gospel seriously and to start caring for the marginalized and the oppressed. I believe He is calling people out of ritual and back into relationship.

... in a very real way the future of the world rests in the hands of local congregations like yours and mine. It's the church or its lights out. Without churches so filled with the power of God that they can't help but spill goodness and peace and love and joy into the world, depravity will win the day; evil will flood the world. But it doesn't have to stay that way. Strong, growing communities of faith can turn the tide of history. They can!

Bill Hybels, *Courageous Leadership*
(Zondervan Publishing House, 2004)

'Oh, I don't reject your Christ. I love your Christ. It's just that so many of you Christians are so unlike your Christ.'

Gandhi

But if we want to be a generation that turns the world upside down, then the revolution has to start with us and it has to start in our hearts. We need to allow our hearts to be opened to the fullness of the gospel – to the 'good news'.

It was whilst I was sharing with those young guys from gangs when I was 18 that I first saw the reality of the gospel. It was not just about stories from the past but it had the power to change lives today. From that point on, God has been doing some serious work on my heart, making me more of the man that He wants me to be.

Active faith

It was my first ever gig and the gutsy guitar interspersed with feedback was driving the crowd wild. It was a dingy venue in north London and the crowd of suspect characters surged forward as the headline act came on. People at the front were pinned against the safety barriers. I watched as my mate negotiated his way to the front of the barriers. He then wrestled his way clear of the crowd and with one swoop of his legs, he was positioned on the edge of the stage lining up his first stage dive of the evening. He made the dive and seemed to be unscathed. He challenged me to go next.

I followed the line he had taken and managed to get past the bouncers, who were now aware of what was going on. Once on the stage I looked out over the crowd that seemed to be jumping in unison to the beat of the drums. Suddenly, I saw it from a very different perspective. As I looked out at the crowd of pierced faces and tattooed-down arms, I hesitated for a moment – unsure if the selection of dubious characters would actually catch me. Perhaps they would just leave me to fall to the bottom of the 'mosh', never to reappear. Aware that the bouncer had pulled himself onto the stage and was now making a beeline for me, it was decision time. I ran to the edge of the stage and launched myself into the air. As I plummeted earthwards, I looked down at the crowd of grungers beneath. Their arms were raised expectantly as my body weight powered into their hands. What a feeling as the crowd not only caught me but passed me along to the edge of the action.

Every day we put our faith in so many things – the bus driver, the kebab shop chef and occasionally even a crowd of grungers. Often we do it without even thinking. Yet when we talk about putting our faith in God, we can get a bit woolly. From quite an early age I have had faith in God but when I read the verse 'faith without deeds is dead'(Jas. 2:26), it made me reconsider what faith is really about. It is very easy to say that we believe in God and understand in our heads what Jesus did on the cross and why, but is this really putting our faith in God?

Chapter 2 of James explains how even the demons believe in God – but this is not a belief that saves. A belief that saves is one of faith which takes control of our lives. We enter into a relationship with God through the free gift of grace. We cannot earn God's love. However, this does not mean that we live lives according to our own agenda. As we begin to know more of God's love, we are spurred on to live a life that produces fruit. This fruit is the evidence of where our faith really is.

Many of us know in our heads that God is trustworthy and faithful but it is sometimes hard to let this knowledge exist as faith in our hearts. In order to help this head knowledge become active faith, it is key that we know God as Father. God has many names in the Bible and Father is one of the most important. The idea of God as Father is often a hard one to understand as many of us have had tough times with our own human dads. As we begin to know God as Father, we can experience faith in our hearts rather than just knowledge in our minds. The fact that Jesus encourages us to pray 'Our Father' shows something of how important it is to know that God loves us and wants to bless us (Mt. 6). As we wrestle with the concept of God as Father, I believe that God increases our faith in Him.

He is unchanging and His promises last for ever. Though the world may change, though governments and regimes may come and go, though nations may rise and fall, God is constant. Therefore He is the Father on whom we can rely. When we put our trust in Him, however, this is no trump card meaning we will never be sick. It does not mean that we will never undergo hardships. But it does mean we can be sure that He will never leave us or give up on us and that nothing can separate us from His love (Rom. 8:38–39).

Prior to that experience at the Salvation Army camp, I had a faith in God but it had not been an active one. It was the kind of faith that meant I would appease my parents by sitting through a church service on occasion. The kind of faith where I tried to be nice and do good as long as I didn't have to put myself out. Yet I had not really grasped what it was to have an active faith whereby I put my faith fully in God. Now, each and every day, I start by giving God my life afresh and putting my faith in Him. When it comes to difficult situations I choose to continue trusting in Him. And as I see Him come through again and again, I am able to take bigger risks for His kingdom and His name.

Ordinary people – extraordinary things

When we truly put our faith in God, we can truly be used by Him. Throughout history God has used ordinary people to do extraordinary things. Too often we look at what we have rather than looking at God. We see ourselves and our gifts, and then we look at the mess the world is in and we crumble at the impossibility of it all. However, Jesus used the boy's five loaves and two fish to feed 5,000 (Lk. 9:13) and in the same way He wants to use the little that we have to bless many. We should not look at the impossibilities but at the enormity of God. Jesus even said that we would do greater things than Him (Jn. 14:12) – what a promise!

We can read in the book of Acts how He used Peter, an ordinary, uneducated fisherman to lead the church. He used David, the youngest of all of his brothers, an ordinary shepherd boy, to become King of Israel. He used Nehemiah, the king's cupbearer to rebuild the walls of Jerusalem. He used Amos the shepherd to prophesy to Israel.

And the amazing thing is that today He is still using ordinary people to do extraordinary things. It is not about how intelligent, how old or how young you are or how you look but it is about being available to God. To be used by God does not mean that you have to be a paid employee of the church or a full-time volunteer but it's about taking your relationship with God into the different aspects of your daily life.

Each week I have approximately 1,000 interactions with young people. I see this as a 1,000 opportunities: a 1,000 opportunities for influence, a 1,000 opportunities for challenge, for provoking, for pushing, for developing, for building, for encouraging and for above all, witnessing.

John, teacher

Refined

In order to be used by God to do these extraordinary things, we need to allow ourselves to be changed by Him, to be refined by Him. We are never the finished article here on earth – we are under construction. We need to allow Him to shape us, mould us and transform us. Society seems to be really keen on the idea of transformation. Daytime TV is made up of hours of programmes that teach us how to transform our home, our garden and even our image. But God does not want to transform our outside – He wants to transform our hearts. God is a God that loves to transform people for His purposes.

> The Lord Jesus cannot live in us fully and reveal himself through us until the proud self within us is broken. This simply means that the hard unyielding self, which justifies itself, wants its own way, stands up for its rights, and seeks its own glory, at last bows its head to God's will, admits it's wrong, gives up its own way to Jesus, surrenders its rights and discards its own glory – that the Lord Jesus might have all and be all. In other words it is dying to self and self-attitudes.
>
> **Roy Hession, *The Calvary Road***
> **(CLC Publications, 2004)**

Peter was a stubborn and impulsive man. He spent three years with Jesus getting it wrong! He told Jesus He didn't need to die. He promised Jesus that he would never deny Him. He used his sword to defend Jesus in the Garden of Gethsemane. His ways simply were not God's ways and he needed to be refined. Just before Jesus is crucified, he denies Him three times and then Jesus looks him in the eye. At that moment he breaks down into tears as he realizes his failings. It's difficult to imagine the thoughts that must have been going through Peter's head during the three days that Jesus was dead.

At this point in history it looked almost impossible that Peter could have fulfilled the promise that Jesus had made at Caesarea Philippi, '… you are Peter, and on this rock I will build my church and the gates of Hades will not overcome it' (Mt. 16:18). Yet after the resurrection, Jesus reinstated Peter asking him three times if he loved Him. Peter had been refined – his own pride had been replaced with a deeper love. Peter then became one of the greatest leaders of all time. At Pentecost, it was Peter who stepped out from among the eleven and it was he who, empowered by the Holy Spirit, preached to see 3,000 new converts. Even Peter's shadow could heal people (Acts 5:15). He led the early church until the day he died, and helped establish the church for all time. Not bad for a refined fisherman!

Moses, too, was a guy that had to be transformed. His passion to see the Israelites freed from their slavery to the Egyptians was clear when he murdered an Egyptian who was flogging an Israelite (Ex. 2:12). But he had taken things into his own hands and it took time before God could use him. His plan of action had been a human one and he spent a staggering forty years being refined by God. When he finally met God in the burning bush, he was in a place called Horeb which literally means 'desolate'. He had fallen from being one of the most powerful men in Egypt to being a shepherd roaming the desert, with a stutter and a stick. At this point God could use him. Moses had been humbled. In God's strength and direction, he freed the Israelites.

Being refined is often a difficult and painful process. God moulds us through the bad as well as the good experiences. His desire is to make us dependent upon Him. I love the parable of the two men, one who builds his house upon rock and the other who builds his house upon sand. When the storm came, only the house on the rock survives because of its strong foundations (Mt. 7:24–29). I think that too often I build my life upon a mixture of sand and rock. Some areas of my life are not built solely upon Christ. It often then takes storms to help me realize new areas in which I need to trust in Him. We need to understand throughout the storms and the good weather that God has our best interests at heart.

God wants every part of us and as we surrender our rights to Him, He is able to use us more effectively. The process of refinement is not a time-limited process where we can one day say that we have been refined. It is a process that takes a lifetime. As a Christian, each day offers new opportunities and challenges – some big and some small –and we must start each day by putting our faith back in God again.

Perspective

As we put more faith in God, we get a new perspective on life. It allows us to engage with the world in a whole new way. As I said earlier, heaven is not the whole deal but it is so important that we know where we are going. When we know our final destination, have read the final chapter and know the end of the story – that Jesus is coming back – our perspective should change. The truth affects the way we live our lives today. C.S. Lewis so wished Christianity wasn't true but had to swallow his pride and put his faith in God.

You must picture me alone in that room in Magdalen, night after night feeling, whenever my mind lifted even for a second from my work, the steady, un-relenting approach of him whom I so earnestly desired not to meet. That which I greatly feared had at last come upon me. In the Trinity Term of 1929 I gave in, and admitted that God was God, and knelt and prayed: perhaps, that night, the most dejected and reluctant convert in all of England.

C. S. Lewis, *Surprised by Joy* (Fount, 2002)

Everyday is a new day
I'm thankful for
Every breath I take
I won't take you for granted
So I learn from my mistakes
It's beyond my control
Sometimes it's best to let go
Whatever happens
In this lifetime
So I trust in love
You have given me
Peace of mind

I feel so alive
For the very first time
I can't deny you
I feel so alive
I feel so alive
For the very first time
And I think I can fly

Sunshine upon my face
A new song for me to sing
Tell the world
How I feel inside
Even though it might
Cost me everything
Now that I know this
So beyond, I can't hold this
I can never
Turn my back away
Now that I've seen you
I can never look away

Now that I know you
(I could never
Turn my back away)
Now that I see you
(I could never look away)
Now that I see you
(I believe no matter
What they say!)

POD *Alive*

I went snowboarding in the Alps with a group of people from all over Europe. We decided to go off-piste and play in the powder. It was day three of a twelve day trip and I was stoked at having the opportunity to improve my skills. We were coming down the side of this mountain and a guy from Austria was leading the way. I thought I could see this jump a little ahead and asked him to check it out for me. He told me to follow his path and I presumed that he meant that if I followed his track I could make it. I turned the board to face downhill and began to pick up speed to hit this jump. My eyes were focused on the Austrian boarder.

As I approached, his face turned from being one of fun into a panicked look that transcended language. As I hit the jump and made stacks of air (well some!), I looked down to see nothing but rocks beneath. I crashed into the jagged rocks and pain flooded my body. I felt sick from the pain but continued to snowboard down the mountain. When I finally made it to the bottom of the gondola, I realized I had hurt my elbow real bad. After an X-ray by a French doctor, I was bandaged up and swallowing painkillers. I had broken my arm. What a thing to do on day three of the trip! It meant no more snowboarding for me for the remaining nine days. D'oh!

Hindsight is a wonderful thing! If I had known the outcome of the jump, my actions would have been very different. I would never have taken one naff jump and sacrificed nine more days of boarding. This story challenges me to think about the eternal outcome of my actions today.

While here on earth, we need to keep this life in perspective. Knowing God should cause us to look at the world framed in eternity. We need to see beyond what the world offers – beyond money, pride, power, sex and fame – to a new age when there will be no more tears and all will worship.

Reality bites

Throughout it all, it is vital that we keep a balance. We mustn't become so super-spiritual that we lose contact with the real world. But at the same time it is just as important that we don't become so embroiled in the things of this world that we forget the bigger picture. Keeping these two ideas in tension is often difficult. Too often we bounce between one and the other, on a rollercoaster of highs and lows.

The following five chapters summarize what I believe are the foundations of what it is to be church. Whenever I meet people who are struggling with their faith, who are in the throws of compromise, I find that there is one of these components missing from their life. Too often we spend time with God when we are 'in the mood' and discipline is often a hated word. It reminds me of detentions at school! But it is discipline that we need – to keep focused and to keep pushing on. In this life it is so easy to become complacent and weary, to think that we are doing 'OK thanks'. Keeping our relationship with God real is essential. We need to keep the communication open and keep getting stuck into the action.

Outnumbered but never outgunned

This call of the church to change the world might seem pretty hardcore. The idea of discipline and surrender can all seem a bit too much. But God equips. As we make this journey towards Him, God will show us grace. Our relationship is not a list of rules with 'Dos and Don'ts'. It is about having freedom in relationship with the Living God.

So, the call is this: wake up church, chase after God, and impact the world. If not you, who? If not now, when?

RECAP

Jesus revolutionaries hear the call

Jesus revolutionaries refuse to compromise

Jesus revolutionaries have an active faith

Jesus revolutionaries do the extraordinary

Jesus revolutionaries are being refined

Jesus revolutionaries understand perspective

Jesus revolutionaries are dedicated

Further Reading

To get started ...

Is That Really You, God?, Loren Cunningham, YWAM Publishing, 2001

Making Jesus Lord, Loren Cunningham, YWAM Publishing, 1989

The Purpose Driven Life, Rick Warren, Zondervan Publishing House, 2003

Radical Christianity, Jim Burns, Regal Books, 1996

In depth ...

Hunger for Reality, George Verwer, Authentic Lifestyle, 1979

Live Like a Jesus Freak, D.C. Talk, Eagle Publishing, 2001

The Kingdom of Jesus, Roger Forster, Authentic Lifestyle, 2002

The Purpose Driven Church, Rick Warren, Zondervan Publishing House, 1996

Wild at Heart, John Eldredge, Thomas Nelson, 2001

my purpose is to further knowledge of You
my vision is to be a vessel
the specifics of why i am where i am
is that actually my business?
if i spend my time wondering why? –
i'll be wasting my time being available
instead i'll trust Your heart
where i cannot see Your hand
i'll rejoice in where i am
because it is You who arranged it
and I will focus on You
because anything else is distraction

MARCY BURNHAM

2

getting biblical

jo wells

I have one of those friends who is super clever but sometimes lacks basic common sense. You know the type of guy, the one that gets straight 'A's but who is always doing something a bit clueless. One day he returned from college and felt hungry. He put the chip pan on the stove and the fat began bubbling away. The telephone then went and my mate left the kitchen to get it. On the phone was one of his friends who invited him to go and buy chips from the chip shop. My mate thought that this was a great idea and left the house in pursuit of some tasty chips.

On his return to the house he began to smell burning and as he came through the front door, he remembered the chip pan that he had left bubbling away. He hurried down the hall and into the kitchen to see the cooker ablaze as was the wall around it. Having noticed this, he closed the kitchen door, walked outside and decided to formulate a plan. The plan was to put the fire out. He went back through the front door, down the hall and into the kitchen, pulling the fire blanket off the wall. By this time, the fire had spread and unsure as to quite how the fire blanket worked, he took it out of the kitchen, down the hall and outside to read the instructions.

Having read the instructions, my mate returned for a third time to find the kitchen completely engulfed in flames – even the clock was on fire! He struggled along on the floor but could hardly see through the smoke and one measly fire blanket was not going to be enough. Admitting defeat, he retreated from the house and called the fire brigade.

Andy Frost

He could have sorted that fire if he had known how to use the fire blanket and then wouldn't have been homeless for two months! So often in our lives we wait until we hit crisis point before we think about reading the instructions. The Bible is the Word of God: 'All Scripture is God-breathed and is useful for teaching, rebuking, correcting and training in righteousness, so that the man of God may be thoroughly equipped for every good work.' (2 Tim. 3:16). The Bible contains everything God wants to say to us. It is our set of instructions for life. Don't wait for a crisis before you take a look at what God has to say.

Setting the scene

For the Word of God is living and active. Sharper than any double-edged sword, it penetrates even to dividing soul and spirit, joints and marrow; it judges the thoughts and attitudes of the heart.

Hebrews 4:12

The author of Psalm 119 was in love with God's Word. He wrote 176 verses expressing love for Scripture. Many people have struggled with God's Word, reading it, understanding it or appreciating it. But when you explore the many different facets of God's Word, you start to glimpse the amazing treasure that God has given us. The Bible is foundational to our relationship with and understanding of God. To dismiss it or allow it to be a dusty ornament on your bookshelf is to disregard God's precious gift. Many people see it as a law book, doling out a list of do's and don'ts. Instead, the psalmist declares that the Word of God is the source of his freedom. Taking time to understand God's Word is so important for us as Christians – we too can fall in love with Scripture.

> In the beginning . . . God said . . .
>
> **Genesis 1:1,3**
>
> **All men are like grass, and all their glory is like the flowers of the field . . . The grass withers and the flowers fall, but the word of our God stands for ever.**
>
> **Isaiah 40:6,8**
>
> From the beginning of time till the end of the world the Word of God stands.

Whenever my family took trips away to visit people, I would sit in the back of the car watching the road signs trying to work out where I was. I would piece together the towns and motorways in my head, as I tried to comprehend the route we were taking. After a long journey my favourite road sign of all had to be 'Rufus Stone – no right turn for 10 miles'. That sign meant *Home* – 10 minutes and I would be out of the car. I would soon be away from my sister, who hated sharing the back seat, and on my way to the most welcome of sights – my bed! It didn't matter where we had been, who we had seen, that sign pointed me home, through the dark to the place where I wanted to be.

So often we leave the Bible untouched in the corner, yet it is our signpost home. In fact, taken as a whole, it is our map from where we are to where we want to be. In part that's why pieces of it may seem so confusing, taken on their own, out of the context of the whole. 'Rufus Stone' probably doesn't mean much to many people, but to me, it points to home because I understand it in relation to the whole journey.

> The word of God is like a mirror in that it shows us who we really are. It is like a map because it shows us where we need to go. It is like a portrait for it paints for us a picture of who God is.
>
> David Wallace (www.jesussite.com)

The Bible contains the story of God and His people. Looking at the map as a whole helps us to understand the individual signposts.

The good news that Jesus brings, the good news that brings all people back into a relationship with God, starts at the beginning of the Bible. Adam and Eve lived in an amazing relationship with God. God would walk with Adam in the Garden of Eden. But Adam and Eve wanted to live their own life, choosing to disobey rather than be dependent on God. So humankind fell. We fell out of relationship with God. All the way through the Old Testament there is a thread of understanding that as hard as Israel tries to be right with God, they will always slip back into living as they desire rather than how God desires. God speaks often of a time when people will be free to live with Him rather than always fighting against the desire to be autonomous. A saviour would be sent to put things right again.

The New Testament heralds this saviour. Jesus Christ lived to show us how to live. Died so that justice is served. And was raised from the dead in victory over the power of Satan and the hold of death. Finally, we are free to be in a stable relationship with God. The letters of the apostles explain how Christ completes and fulfils the promises of God found in the Old Testament. They teach us how to live in the freedom found in Christ and how to share the good news with others.

The Bible is the complete history of God and His creation. Understanding it in its entirety reveals God's heart and His message for the world to return to and remain in Him.

The Bible doesn't just contain history, it also paints the most awesome picture of God and His character. The God of the Old Testament is often seen as one of judgement and of anger. Yet in the New Testament He is called Loving Father. It sometimes seems as if the two parts are talking about two different Gods. But as you delve deeper into the story of God, you see His characteristics are consistent and prevalent throughout.

The portrait of God infuses the most exciting stories you could read about. Think the Bible is boring? How about this then …

- Erotic sex poetry (Song)
- Bloodiest deaths (Judg. 3:16–25)
- Murder and deception (Gen. 34)
- Horror film style miracles (Ezek. 37)

God raises up people just like you and me and gets them doing the randomest of things. Ezekiel got to eat food cooked over cow manure (Ezek. 4:1–17). Baalam had a conversation with a donkey (Num. 22:26–31). Paul healed people by sending them his handkerchief (Acts 19:12). And John was taken into the very realm of heaven (Rev. 19:11). Reading the Bible cannot be dull when you grasp something of this awesome unpredictable God who wants to take us on an amazing adventure with Him.

Where's the sense in that?

When I was eleven, my humanities teacher taught us the most basic principle. He told us that hot air rises and cold air sinks. I cannot remember a time when I didn't know that. It is one of life's basic facts, kinda like the one about the world being round. However, I had a question. If hot air rises and cold air sinks, and if the principle that air circulates, i.e. it's the same air molecules that move around, is correct, then how does that hot air get cold so that it sinks? Where does the heat go?

My teacher couldn't answer me. He had never thought about it. For three weeks I refused to believe that hot air rises and cold air sinks, because no-one could answer my question. I couldn't understand why so many people just blindly accepted something that they could not explain. Finally, three weeks later, a science teacher explained to me that the heat comes from the vibrations between the molecules. The further away from the earth the molecules travel the greater the distance between them, therefore less vibrations, less heat and they sink. I could, at last, know that what I had been taught was indeed true. I wasn't blindly believing something with no understanding. It had been explained to me and made logical sense.

The Bible tells us that there is a reason for our hope and faith (1 Pet. 3:15). Yet often we ignore the problems that arise from believing the Bible is God's truth. We stick our head in the sand and hope that no-one will ask us questions. Often we're too scared to acknowledge them ourselves.

The Word of God in the words of men.

> Josh McDowell, *Reasons Skeptics Should Consider Christianity* (Here's Life Publishers)

The Bible is God's Word written through humans. It is a partnership. Many people query the validity of the Bible because of the contradictions between different writers. For example, there is a clear contradiction found in 2 Kings 24:8 and 2 Chronicles 36:9. In the passage in Kings, Jehoiachin is recorded as reigning for three months and in Chronicles, he is said to have reigned for three months and ten days. This error is probably because the author of Kings was writing about Israel's relationship with God. He would probably have rounded up the length of the reign, not seeing it as integral. The writer of Chronicles, on the other hand, was giving a socio-economic historical account and was more concerned with factual detail.

As we read the Bible there are slight errors but for me this helps me know that this is not some made-up book. The range of writers from fishermen to kings, from shepherds to leaders enhances the beauty and cultural richness of the Bible. All of these writers share the same message though they are writing across different centuries and in different nations. That is amazing.

The minor errors show that there has been no great cover up. Our responsibility as Christians is not to ignore the difficulties or make up excuses for them. Instead we are to grapple with issues concerning the validity of the Bible.

Freestyle

The Bible must be the invention either of good men or angels, bad men or devils, or of God. However, it was not written by good men, because good men would not tell lies by saying 'Thus saith the Lord', it was not written by bad men because they would not write about doing good duty, while condemning sin, and themselves to hell; thus, it must be written by divine inspiration.

Charles Wesley, *Josh McDowell: Evidence That Demands a Verdict* (Authentic Media, 2004)

Muslims recognize Christians as 'People of the Book'. Our faith and knowledge of God is founded on what the Old Testament says. Yet today many people discount the Bible's worth and its meaning because they are unwilling to work at understanding it. It's often easier to replace God's Word with our own common sense.

The Bible explains God's point of view. His insight must be greater than ours – after all He is God! So why do we presume that we know better than the Word of God? Can our common sense reveal and destroy the devil's schemes? Can our common sense reveal God's will and purpose in our lives and the lives of those around us?

The Word of God well understood and religiously obeyed is the shortest route to spiritual perfection. And we must not select a few favourite passages to the exclusion of others. Nothing less than a whole Bible can make a whole Christian.

A.W. Tozer, *Of God and Men* (Christian Publications, 1960)

The Bible speaks

I became a Christian because of a prophecy that someone spoke over me. A stranger came up to me and spoke about things that he could not have known without the help of God. I was utterly confused and outside of my experience. I didn't know where to go in my past to tell me how to process what had happened. So I prayed. 'God if you can speak to me through other people, then you can speak to me through the Bible. What do I do with this?!' I opened my Bible and prayed that God would direct me to something that might help. I turned straight to a passage I had never read before. '… no prophecy of Scripture came about by the prophet's own interpretation … but men spoke from God as they were carried along by the Holy Spirit.' (2 Pet. 1:20–21). I sat in a dingy coffee shop in Skegness and cried. God was real and had spoken to me!

There are times when reading the Bible that God speaks straight into our lives. It almost feels as if the verses were written thousands of years ago simply so we could read it in the situation we find ourselves in today. A verse leaps out at you, and you know that is God's Word for you.

> I went home, and every morning and afternoon I ate and drank nothing. Every evening I ate just one small bowl of steamed rice. I cried like a hungry child, to His heavenly Father, wanting to be filled with His Word. For the next one hundred days I prayed for a Bible. Until I could bear it no more.
>
> **Brother Yun, *The Heavenly Man*
> (Monarch Publications, 2002)**

But there is a danger in adopting this practice as the norm. Misunderstandings will result if we interpret

Scripture as one-dimensional. Have you ever been told that the Bible is a 'Love letter from God to you'? Unfortunately that isn't the whole story. The Bible is a collection of books written by different people, to different audiences at different times in different places. To read and appreciate the Bible in its entirety is to know the revelation of God. The way the Bible comes truly alive is by appreciating its context. If you understand why it was written in the first place it helps you grasp the truth that exists in it today.

All Scripture is God-breathed – not just the bits you like or agree with. The bits that make you feel uncomfortable are just as godly as the passages that are all fluffy and nice. Those difficult passages begin to make sense when you understand why they were written. Should all women be silent in church or were there a bunch of noisy women interrupting church meetings in Ephesus who needed dealing with? If you were to pick up a mathematician's PhD thesis and started reading it, the likelihood is you wouldn't understand a word of it. You would need to read up on some basic maths first to try and understand the principles. You would have to devote some time, study and seek advice in order to understand what it is you're reading. Why do we assume that the Bible will make instant sense? It requires study – we must read commentaries and ask questions. Knowledge will lead to understanding.

A few years ago an American politician tried to deny that the Holocaust had ever happened. He claimed that it was a fabrication and we had all been duped by the media. His claims caused phenomenal outrage. People couldn't believe that he had the audacity to say such things. There were still people alive that had been tortured in the concentration camp by the Nazis. Survivors knew the Holocaust was fact. No-one believed that it was all a lie when the eyewitnesses were still around.

Peter defended the gospel accounts and the claims of Jesus Christ saying: 'We did not follow cleverly invented stories when we told you about the power and coming of our Lord Jesus Christ, but we were eye-witnesses of His majesty … We ourselves heard this voice that came from heaven when we were with Him on the sacred mountain.' (2 Pet. 1:16–18). His argument being 'I was there, this is Truth!'

Promises fulfilled

A couple of months after I became a Christian I was sitting in a Christian bookshop having a coffee with a mate. On the wall was a description of the crucifixion. Every word spoke of what Jesus went through on that fateful day. Yet as I read on, I saw that Isaiah was credited as the author – 700 years before Christ. The cynic in me laughed. How ridiculous was it that we needed to fabricate prophecy about Jesus? Isaiah couldn't have written such an accurate description of Jesus' death 700 years before He was even born! Then I went home and opened my Bible to Isaiah 53. I couldn't believe my eyes. Everything that was predicted had happened. How could anyone reading this not believe Jesus was the Son of God?

Jesus fulfils the promises and prophecies of Scripture; it's reckoned there are over 300 prophecies in the Old Testament that point to Jesus Christ. Sometimes the story itself is the prophecy such as in the case of Jonah (Mt. 12:40). Sometimes there are direct predictions made like those found in Isaiah (Is. 9:6). Throughout the Old Testament the life, death and resurrection of Jesus are foretold in a variety of ways.

Sanctify them by the Truth, your word is Truth.

John 17:17

As Scripture affirms Jesus, so Jesus affirms Scripture. He quoted scripture during His temptation, at His commissioning and throughout His teaching. He also quoted scripture to predict His own death and resurrection. Jesus declared Scripture to be truth (Jn. 17:17). Therefore Scripture is validated by the highest possible source – God Himself!

While I was studying at university I met many people who knew the Bible far better than I did. They lectured on it every week, their life's study had been dedicated to the Bible, and yet they weren't Christians. I couldn't understand it. How could you read the Bible and not find truth? How could you read about Jesus and not realize that He is your Saviour? How could you read about sin, heaven and hell and not want to be reunited with God? How could anyone read the Bible and not be changed? I began to see that the problem was that every academic I met was reading the Bible as a piece of literature or as a historical source. They weren't reading it as the living Word of God and therefore they weren't asking the Living God to speak to them through it. The truth is that the Holy Spirit communicates through His Word, so if we aren't inviting the Holy Spirit to be with us as we read the Bible, it will become just another book. The absence of God while reading His Word is what makes it difficult and a chore to read. And so, it's such a simple principle, just pray before you begin reading 'God what do you want to speak to me about today?' Let Him direct you through His Word, and allow His wisdom to permeate your thoughts.

A friend of mine once got so hooked on reading the Bible. He started reading the book of Samuel and suddenly began to see how the Bible fitted together. He challenged himself to read the whole Bible in five months. Taking his Bible everywhere, he read it over breakfast, in break times, even in the car. Amazingly he finished it all in three months.

When I hear someone ask a Christian what the Bible says and the Christian doesn't know, I feel ashamed. We declare that the Bible is foundational to our faith, and yet many of us haven't even read it all the way through. Falling in love with God's Word may seem like a really strange concept, but God's Word is a beautiful gift to us. However, we often feel that reading it is like a dreaded piece of homework that we spend all our time avoiding. God promises to write His law on our hearts (Jer. 31:33). But we need to actually read it first.

Fisticuffs

A friend of mine once asked me if I got up every morning prepared to fight, because if I wasn't prepared to fight I might as well stay in bed! Matthew 11:12 says: 'The kingdom of heaven has been forcefully advancing, and forceful men lay hold of it.' We are in a battle. In Revelation we're told '... woe to the earth ... because the devil has gone down to you! He is filled with fury, because he knows that his time is short.' (Rev. 12:12). In other words, he knows he's going down and boy is he going to make sure he takes as many as he can with him!

Knowing Scripture isn't enough. It isn't for us then to leave it on the bookshelf, pat ourselves on the back, congratulating ourselves that we have read it. We are to use it!

Every time I do something stressful, whether it's sitting an exam, going to a meeting, or going travelling, I have a panicky dream the night before. I dream that I will forget something, or not have thought of something. Exams – what if I am supposed to bring the book with me? What if there is a section I haven't studied that everybody else knew about? Holidays – what if I turn up at the airport without any money or without my passport? I lie there all night, my mind running through everything I haven't done and all the things that could go wrong and how I could remedy them. I get up in the morning, not only ridiculously stressed, but now also exhausted! I fear being under-prepared all the time.

Ephesians 6 says: 'Finally, be strong in the Lord and in his mighty power. Put on the full armour of God so that you can take your stand against the devil's schemes.' (Eph. 6:10–11). The vast majority of the armour is protective – shield, breastplate, helmet. The only weapon as a Christian you are given is the Sword of the Spirit – which is the Word of God. The Bible is your weapon – with it you are prepared to fight, without it you are lost.

Jesus fought Satan. They had an almighty struggle in the desert to see who was going to have the ultimate power. Would Satan fall to Jesus, or would Jesus bow to Satan?

Jesus won. To every temptation Satan threw at Him, He always responded with scripture. Satan could not stand against Scripture, and fled (Lk. 4:1–13). There is no argument against Scripture, no room for debate. Satan has no purity in him, and the Bible is the pure Word of God, the two cannot co-exist, therefore one must leave – and it will always be Satan (Jas. 4:7).

> **The Devil fears the Word of God, He can't bite it; it breaks his teeth.**
>
> **Martin Luther**

There is a famous quote that states 'the devil's greatest achievement is convincing the world that he doesn't exist'.

So often as Christians we forget him, and we need to be reminded that Peter commands us to 'Be self-controlled and alert. Your enemy the devil prowls around like a roaring lion looking for someone to devour.' (1 Pet. 5:8). The devil does exist, and he doesn't like you – you are his enemy and he is fighting you with everything he's got. But we already have the victory, Jesus defeated him at the cross, and we live in that victory. He is no threat to you if you stand firm. Equip yourself with the knowledge of Scripture. Satan is terrified of it – because with it you can defeat him. He will therefore try everything to stop you from reading it!

A friend of mine has built herself the full armour of God. She has the helmet, the breastplate, the footwear – everything. Of all the pieces she chooses to give to others to start their own armour collection, she always gives them a sword. You fight from day one, so be prepared!

Give me wisdom

> Always remember what is written in the Book of the Teachings. Study it day and night to be sure to obey everything that is written there. If you do this you will be wise and successful in everything.
>
> Joshua 1:8 (NCV)

Joshua was not in a good place. He had been second to Moses for forty years. He had seen God do amazing things through Moses for his people. He was at the parting of the Red Sea, and witnessed God save Israel. He had accompanied Moses up Mount Sinai and saw the glory of God descend like a cloud. He was present when God gave

Moses the law and the covenant. At every landmark of the Exodus, Joshua was there – watching at the sidelines.

And now it was his turn. He must have been bricking it! As Joshua saw it, Moses was God's guy, not him. How could Joshua be expected to follow such an amazing leader? God is careful to make sure that Joshua knows the score. The opening chapter of Joshua is all about what God, not Joshua, is going to do. The only direct action God commands Joshua to do is to study His Word. That's the key! Knowledge of the Word will lead to wisdom and success. It's a principle we forget all too easily these days.

> Brothers, stop thinking like infants . . . in your thinking be adults.
>
> **1 Corinthians 14:20**

When I first became a Christian I dragged up a distant memory from Sunday school that said one of God's favourite prayers in the Bible is that of Solomon and his plea for wisdom. God was so impressed with his humility that He granted him not only wisdom but wealth and honour as well. (Check it out in 1 Kgs. 3:5–15). So I thought to myself that maybe it would be a good thing for me to pray for wisdom, too.

So, every day, I would pray 'God, give me the gift of wisdom. Give me knowledge of you and your heart so I might share it with others.' Now these sort of prayers never get answered by waking up the next morning and discovering you are the Christian version of the Dalai Lama, but gradually you notice that you know what to say in a difficult situation. You hear God's voice, and can speak advice to someone. There is wisdom in your character that wasn't there before.

The thing about praying for wisdom is that you don't simply acquire it – it is imparted to you. Wisdom isn't something you simply get, but something passed on. Every day that I prayed for wisdom I read and remembered the Bible. Instead of attending church and forgetting everything that had happened the moment I left, the sermons remained with me. I could quote Bible verses that I had only heard once before to people. And the sermons and the readings would always be perfectly timed for when I would need to use them. God was imparting His wisdom to me as and when I needed it. All of it came from the Bible. If you want to influence others around you, if you want God's Word to benefit your surroundings, learn His Word. The Bible contains God's wisdom. Wisdom is a gift God wants to give us: seek it, God will not deny His children a good thing (Ps. 84:11).

God takes us all on a journey, constantly leading us closer to Him. Every day He reveals more of Himself to us, more of His heart, His will for our lives. He gives us the gifts that we need and that we seek. The Bible is our means to that revelation. He might use other people, creation, silence or His voice to speak to us, but the permanent source of God's revelation comes through His Word.

Swimming in the river and digging the well

There are times in life when you may get those awesome collective experiences. You're at a massive conference listening to a great worship band. The speaker goes through God's Word, and you encounter God and hear Him in a way you never do back at home. These are the streams of God's living water. You get refreshed and encouraged – it's all handed to you on a plate. The thing is it's really easy living waiting for the next opportunity for the stream to flow past you again. I call this being a

weekend conference junkie. You have the crash about three
weeks after you get home, 'cos the world has infiltrated the
Christian bubble that was created while you were away.
So, depressed that you can't cope any more, all your heart
wants to do is return to where it was safe, where it was easy
and everything made sense. The trouble is that as good as
the experience was, God wants us to go deeper with Him.
The streams are great but they are short-lived. Sometimes
God asks us to dig wells. Digging is hard work, often
seemingly thankless. You just end up repetitively shifting
dirt. But once the well is finished you have a permanent
source of God's water in your life. It takes discipline and
dedication. It would be so much easier just to hang about
waiting for someone else to tell you what to think and
what you need to know but Peter commands us to do it
ourselves. Be like adults. As my mate realized having not
read the fire blanket instructions, life will side-swipe you
when you are least expecting it. Wisdom and preparation
are the keys to successful living. Life in Christ is about
work. Working to keep on track.

And the Truth will set you free

One of the names given to Satan is the father of Lies (Jn.
8:44). He lies all the time, especially to us and especially
about who we are. He is our accuser – he condemns us
before God, he desperately wants us to lose our way.

A preacher once said that the devil's tactic used to be
to kill Christians, so that they couldn't fight him. But he
has discovered that it is far more effective to simply render
them incapable of doing anything, by telling them lies.
Sometimes Satan uses our insecurities: 'You're useless',
'You're ugly', 'You're stupid'. Other times he will attack
us with pride: 'Well done me', 'I'm the best'. Neither
reflect the identity we have in Christ. If we believe these

thoughts that Satan puts our way then we are not living life in obedience to Christ. Satan's lies are the opposite of what God tells us about ourselves in the Bible.

There are amazing promises written about you in the Bible. God's Word to us is peppered with declarations about our identity, our purpose, our future and our relationship with our Creator. And yet so often we choose to ignore God's promises over us in favour of Satan's lies.

> The weapons we fight with are not the weapons of this world. On the contrary, they have divine power to demolish strongholds. We demolish arguments and every pretension that sets itself up against the knowledge of God, and we take captive every thought to make it obedient to Christ.
>
> **2 Corinthians 10:4–5**

The actions you produce show the attitudes you have adopted. A friend of mine was constantly putting herself down. She didn't even notice that she was doing it half the time, 'Oh I couldn't do that.' 'I don't deserve that opportunity, I'm not good enough.' 'No-one could like me, I'm ugly' and so it went on. Because of the lies she never pushed herself forward, she was negative about herself and others, she grew depressed, and she became less and less like the person she actually was. Desperate to return to her true identity she began to fight the lies in her life. It took her a while but every time she noticed she was saying a lie about herself she refuted it. 'I am good enough "For we are God's workmanship, created in Christ Jesus to do good works, which God prepared in advance for us to do"' (Eph. 2:10). 'I'm not ugly, "God saw all that he had made, and it was very good"' (Gen. 1:31). Gradually, she started to live in confidence. She learnt who she was in Christ, to trust the promises she read in the Bible, and to recognize when Satan was trying to get her to stumble. The Word of God set her free. She was no longer held by the lies and curses she had spoken over herself, she was free to live in Christ.

Break the curse that you live under. Look at what the Bible says about you and then look at what you say about yourself. Which one should be brought into accordance with the other?

This Living Word is waiting for you. Read it. It is powerful against our enemies. It is foundational to our faith. There is nothing greater. There is nothing more precious than the gift of God's Word to us. Where you have found it dry or boring, ask God to breathe life into it. When you are rooted in His Word you will be rooted in Him.

RECAP

The Bible is God's Word

The Bible contains our instructions

The Bible makes sense

The Bible is true

The Bible needs to be read

The Bible is our sword

Practical tips

- Read the same passage in different translations to see how they are similar and how they are different. Get hold of *THE MESSAGE* or the *Street Bible* for some radical differences!

- Re-write letters in modern language or even as text messages. What is the writer really trying to get across?

- Every time you come to read a passage, begin by praying that God would reveal Himself through His Word. Read through a passage and ask 'What does it say about – me, God, Satan?'

- Create a Word area in your home. Put Bibles in there, pens, paper, clay, devotional books anything that might help you understand and appreciate the Word. Make it comfortable – with cushions and pictures – and a place that you would want to spend time in. A place where you can relax and enjoy spending time focusing on God.

- Journal your Bible reading. Make notes of what you've read and what it has spoken to you about. Refer back to it and seek God in the passage and messages you've recorded.

- Create memory cards with key bits of the Bible – this is especially good for learning some of God's promises. Keep them in your pocket and have a flick through them when you are sat at a bus-stop or waiting for a friend.

- Re-write the story from one of the character's points of view. Put yourself in their position and imagine you are living in biblical times.

- If you're not much of a reader, then all this talk of reading and studying the Bible might well fill you with a sense of dread. So why don't you try and create what you're looking at in the Bible in a form of artwork, draw it, sculpt it. Create whatever helps you express the Word of God in a way that is relevant to you.

- Read a section of Psalm 119 every day for a week. What aspects seem strange to you? What do you disagree with? What surprises you about what the writer says? Ask God to let you fall in love with His Word.

- Shut yourself in your room. The Bible is full of drama so enact what you read. Speak it out aloud. The poetry of the psalms or the urgency of the gospels come alive. A lot of the Bible was originally meant as spoken text so speak it and look at it in a new light.

- Build yourself a Bible mobile with promises of God in different sections or write your identity in Christ on the mirror. Every day you will remind yourself of who you are in Christ and begin your day with God at the forefront of your thoughts.

- Have lots of open Bibles around your house or bedroom. Every time you pass one read a verse to season your life with Scripture.

- Go on-line and buy some CDs of the spoken Bible – sit back, chill out and listen to the Word.

Further reading

To get started ...

Buy a concordance that matches your translation, for example:

The NIV complete Concordance, Edward W. Goodrick and John R. Kohlenberger, Hodder & Stoughton Religious, 1994

The Bible Speaks Today series, Edited by J.A. Motyer and John R.W. Stott, InterVarsity Press

The Street Bible, Rob Lacey, Zondervan Publishing House, 2002

THE MESSAGE: REMIX (The Bible in Contemporary Language), Eugene H. Peterson, Navpress, 2003

Cover to Cover, Selwyn Hughes and Trevor J. Partridge, CWR

The Bible for Blockheads, Douglas Connelly, Zondervan Publishing House, 1999

In depth ...

Victory over the Darkness, Neil T. Anderson, Monarch Publications, 2002

Understanding the Bible, John Stott, Scripture Union Publishing, 2003

Celebration of Discipline, Richard Foster, Hodder & Stoughton Religious, 1999

How to Read the Bible for All Its Worth, Gordon D. Fee and Douglas Stuart, Scripture Union, 2001

Through trials and tribulations, hard times and congratulations.
Through all the phases and reservations, ignore the lies and character assassinations
I sing your praises, in public places, 'cause your love's so real that I can almost taste it.
So I embrace it, life is a struggle but with you, I can face it.
Your name I raise it, but the haters try to replace it.
'Jesus' the very definition of Love only a foolish man would forsake it.
I'm taking small steps slowly stumbling towards my creator.
So in the face of this world I will continue to labour.
Not be dictated to and always try to love my neighbour
And I will savour, every moment in your presence.
Trample on my fear and grip the mic. without hesitance
The eternal residence, my minds fixed and firmly focused.
Where there is room for the weak, the lost, the trampled and the hopeless.
So in the midst of joy, or the dry times when I'm broken
I shout your name Lord with every breath, thought, action and emotion.

MC McGLADIUS, 'Shout your name', from the album 'Full Time'
www.29thchapter.org.uk

hymns and psalms

andy frost

It was a chilly, yet incredibly bright, January morning. I pulled up at Fistral Beach to see the waves piling up on the golden sand. I immediately knew it was big as the sound of the barrelling surf echoed into the car. Transfixed by the view of perfect waves stacked up on the horizon and full of excitement I scrambled to get my wetsuit on. It was really big. As I gave my board a quick wax, I left the road and began to jog towards the beach. As I reached the sand, I realized just how big it was. My jog turned into a slow walk, then a meander and then I just stopped and watched the waves pounding the shoreline.

My excitement was quickly replaced with fear as I watched the mountains of water head landward. The beach was filling up slowly with other dawn surfers and stray dog-walkers. I stood there up to my head in rubber, pondering whether I really should go in. I couldn't just return to the car – I would look like such a fool.

I walked up to the ocean's edge and placed my feet cautiously in the water – instantly feeling the frosty reception. With a deep intake of breath I jumped into the icy ocean and paddled out over the waves. The thought of imminent death kept pacing through my head. 'It's only water' I kept thinking to myself. I use it to brush my teeth and make tea – can it really be that dangerous?

Having spent a while paddling around and watching the swell, I went for it – dropping in on what seemed like an 80-foot wave. The board bounced down the face of the wave and I lost control, plunging into the depths of the ocean. The wave rolled me around like I was on a washing machine cycle and my lungs burned as I desperately held my breath. It felt like a lifetime spent waiting to breathe and then I suddenly popped to the surface to see the next wave breaking directly on top of me. I was sucked back under and once again I struggled to get back to the surface. My heart was beating so fast, my head was hurting from the cold and my lungs were gagging for breath. Finally I came back to the surface. I pulled in my leash to find only half of my surfboard. The wave had snapped the board in two.

Most surfers have had one or more close calls out in big surf. I have stuck the half board on my bedroom wall to remind me of just how powerful water can be! It is so easy to underestimate its power.

Andy Frost

Worship – it's a God thing

It is also easy to underestimate God. In my walk with Him, I have often misunderstood who He is – there are times when I recognize His loving side and try to box Him in. I have a warm fuzzy feeling and forget the incomprehensible enormity of He who loves me. There are other times when I focus too much on His power and not enough on His love. I see God as being some distant force rather than an intimate friend. Many people who don't know Christ have this understanding of God. They picture Him as a geezer sat on a cloud that occasionally sends down thunderbolts, rarely concerned with His creation. People decide not to worship Him – after all what has He done for them?

> The man who cannot wonder, who does not habitually wonder and worship, is but a pair of spectacles behind which there is no eye.
>
> **Thomas Carlyle**

I believe God needs to be worshipped simply because of who He is. His very existence demands it. When worshipping we need to recognize the two sides of His character – the Omnipotent Creator and the Intimate Friend. When we ignore an aspect of God, we belittle Him and our worship falls short. We need to become a people that can hold these mind-blowing concepts in tension rather than worshipping from a purely human, logical perspective.

> Amazing Grace, how sweet the sound
> That saved a wretch like me ...
> I once was lost but now am found,
> Was blind, but now, I see
>
> **Thomas Newton**

Whenever I surf a wave or stand on the top of a mountain or watch the stars, I marvel at creation. I marvel at its enormity and beauty. It's then that I see the vastness of God – the Artistic Creator!

In the book of Romans (1:20), Paul writes '... since the creation of the world God's invisible qualities – His eternal power and divine nature – have been clearly seen, being understood from what has been made ...' Every day we see something of God's creation – even in today's urban environments. Something of God can be seen in the trees, the sky, and even in our own bodies. Yet we seem to miss these as opportunities to meet with God. Life moves too fast. We need to slow down and take time out. Rather than rushing to study or work, spend time appreciating this incredible world in which we live – taking notice of the seasons and allowing God to speak.

Worship is about recognizing God's enormity and His glory. Isaiah 6 captures the essence of a human meeting God. Isaiah comes face-to-face with the glory of God and has a vision of the Lord sat on a throne with His robe filling the temple. His reaction is to fall flat on his face, yelling, 'Kill me now, I'm doomed!' What a reaction! How often do we glimpse something of God and fall to our faces? Yet when we begin to see God and His glory, we realize just how insignificant we really are in comparison!

A friend of mine experienced a vision like this. He was stood in the service worshipping when he suddenly fell to the floor. People from around the church building rushed over convinced he was ill! He had in fact grasped something of God's glory and was overcome by the experience. It was quite surreal watching him explain that he wasn't sick but that he had just seen a vision of God. People in the service just did not expect that kind of thing to happen and they couldn't comprehend it.

My mate had opened himself up to seeing something more of God. I have never had a 'falling-to-the-floor-vision' experience but I grasp something more of God's glory whenever I take risks. As I entered the surf that morning, I was taking a risk. When we enter God's presence, how often does it feel that we are being risky? Risky worship is an expression of abandonment and asking God for more. If we really want to know more of God's glory, we need to make our worship more uncomfortable and push ourselves out of our comfort zones. Perhaps too much of our corporate worship prevents God from moving – perhaps the meetings we have reflect the orderly experiences that we feel comfortable with rather than the Isaiah-type experience that turns the world upside down. I encourage you to take risks and ask God to show more of Himself to you.

The Jews knew the risks associated with entering into God's presence. The Holy of Holies was the most sacred place in all the temple, for that was where the presence of God dwelt. The high priest alone was allowed to enter and only after a vast and complicated series of purification rituals. According to Jewish tradition, the priest would have a rope tied around his ankle as he entered the Holy of Holies in case he died when encountering God's glory. The rope would then be used to pull him out – nice! God is HOLY. Can we even begin to grasp how perfect, how different and set apart He is?

However, above all of God's holiness, power and might, God is love. 1 John 4:16 shows us that love is His very essence. This is not some pink, fluffy valentine love. His love way exceeds our human understanding.

> So you are no longer a slave but a son; and since you are a son, God has made you also an heir.
>
> **Galatians 4:7**

I love the old hymn 'Amazing Grace' because it speaks of the immense love that God has for us. The Jews understood the notion of sin and what it was that separated us from God. They understood that they could never get to God, no matter how hard they tried, no matter what they did. They knew sin would always get in the way. But at the cross, sin was paid for. At the cross we have been set free – forgiven. That which we could not do for ourselves, Jesus did for us. Why? Because God is love.

God did not stop with forgiveness either! The most amazing thing is that He desires a relationship with us. More than that, He adopts us as His sons and daughters. Since time began God has wanted a relationship with us; He walked with Adam in the Garden of Eden, and now thanks to the cross, He can walk with us today. No longer do we have to go through priests and rituals to get to God, but we can approach the 'throne of grace' as sons and daughters, in other words, with confidence (Heb. 4:16). We are back where we were always supposed to be.

Creation shows us so much of God but it is through the cross that we are really able to grasp His character. The cross shows us His mercy, His humility, His power, His faithfulness, and most importantly, His love. God deserves worship for who He is in His very being. We should not worship Him out of fear but out of adoration for the King of Creation and the King of Love. It is when we put these two aspects of God together, that we can fully understand why it is that we must worship Him.

We worship one God. We have spoken lots about God the Father deserving our worship but we should also praise Jesus. In a world where Jesus is either known as a swear word or a nice bloke, we as Christians need to be announcing Him in our worship as Lord, King, God. After all, one day every knee will bow and every tongue will confess that Jesus is Lord (Phil. 2:10).

Worship – *it's what we're made for*

As we worship, we glimpse something more of God and as we do so, we enter a time of confession that allows us to get right with God.

However, it is so easy to take the cross for granted. Confession can become a piece of liturgy or an airy-fairy concept. Worse still, we can become satisfied with where we are with God and content with certain sin. This is especially true when we begin comparing ourselves with others rather than Jesus. As we worship, we need to take our eyes off those around us and start focusing afresh on Him – it is then that we grasp what we are really like – in comparison to perfection. A true reality check!

One of the funniest things to watch is someone who thinks that they are pretty smooth walk past an infrared light. Suddenly they don't look quite so cool when their fake tan and dandruff is nicely illuminated! Not so cool – eh? As we enter God's presence, it is like looking at ourselves in an infrared light. We suddenly see the blemishes and the shortcomings in our lives. Confession keeps us humble! It reminds *us* of just who we are and allows us to put things behind us, move closer to God and make sure that He is being given the glory He deserves.

I hear you ask 'But how do I know when there is something wrong in my life?' Well, I get that tugging feeling on my heart as the Holy Spirit highlights an area of my life that is less than honourable. It is important that we understand that God convicts and does not condemn. Condemnation is feeling guilty but not being sure quite what is wrong. Conviction is when God highlights a specific area of our lives that we need to sort out. It can often come as a thought that pops into your head. As you sort it, you are able to make Him first again and His peace returns to your heart.

Sorting it out is more than saying a quick 'sorry' and then repeating the action. It is about repentance – the word means a turn about in direction, moving the opposite way. It involves a change in heart for, ultimately, God desires that we have a pure heart. Check out Psalm 51:10 – 'Create in me a pure heart, O God, and renew a steadfast spirit within me'. But what does this pure heart mean in reality? As we are washed clean, how does this affect our worship?

I ran a guys' weekend and we had about fifty young men looking at lad issues. It came to the end of our time together when suddenly God's presence filled the room in such a powerful way. Many of us got to our knees and began confessing. Big guys knelt crying in repentance – it was quite a sight!

Worship – one big sing-song?

In the church today, worship and singing are normally seen as being one and the same. Singing songs is definitely a key aspect of worship (Eph. 5:19). The first song in the Bible comes as early as Exodus as the Israelites leave Egypt, then there is the book of Psalms full of songs of worship and finally the picture in Revelation is of people from every nation singing praise in unison. There is something indescribably powerful as believers sing together with one voice. Some of my most tangible God-experiences have come during song-singing worship.

I hope that as a generation we will continue to use music in praise but I hope that we can branch out into other music styles, too. It saddens me that we have such a limited selection of music genres used in worship. I long for a time when we will see people expressing worship in different ways – when urban culture will see the church worshipping corporately with hip hop and break dance, when rock culture will see stage-diving as praise to Jesus and when classical music, poetry and jazz will offer a wider array of worship celebrations. We need to break away from being so monotone – surely God created us to express our worship with variety?

However, worship is bigger than singing alone. Perhaps sometimes we put too much emphasis on song. Jesus is never recorded as teaching the disciples the importance of singing and I fear that our big 'worship' events at festivals and conferences become too much about the music and the experience – putting ourselves rather than Jesus at the centre. It scares me to hear people walk out of events and say 'I didn't think much of the worship'. Are we forgetting that worship is not for us but for God and that any blessing that we receive from the activity is merely a bonus?

> When the music fades,
> All is stripped away,
> And I simply come;
> Longing just to bring something that's of worth
> That will bless Your heart.
>
> I'll bring you more than a song
> For a song in itself
> Is not what you have required.
> You search much deeper within
> through the way things appear
> You're looking into my heart
>
> Matt Redman,
> *The Unquenchable Worshipper*, 2002

Our daily lives should become worship. Let's kick the habit of saying 'Now let's have a time of worship'.

Worship is not something that we plug in and out of. We need to stop boxing areas of our lives and allow God into everything! The word worship has Anglo-Saxon roots and comes from the word 'worthship' – giving something of worth to God. What do we have of worth?

One of the most powerful acts of worship in the New Testament for me is the woman with the alabaster jar of perfume. The woman breaks all the etiquette of the day and enters the place where Jesus is sat. She then cracks open a jar of expensive perfume – probably the most valuable thing she owned – and anoints Jesus. Jesus' feet would have been gross from the dust and the manure of the road, yet she cleans them. Not with water and a cloth but with her tears and her hair. She offered that which was most precious to her. She offered her worldly wealth and her pride. What gift can you give to Him?

Nothing is more valuable to Him than you. God wants you, warts and all. Worship is about putting Jesus first. It is about saying 'here I am' and 'I give myself to you'.

Singing is therefore not enough. God wants more than Sunday morning choruses and songs. In fact, many of the prophets spoke of God's anger at hypocritical worship. For example, Amos spoke out against Israel and the people's religious behaviour that was not backed up by their daily lives. They were performing religious rituals on one hand whilst worshipping idols and quashing the poor on the other. God has given us our lives to worship Him with – this is what we were created for!

What is in our hearts needs to be expressed as worship in schools, in the workplace and even on the football pitch! Each section of our lives becomes worship when we dedicate it to Jesus. We need to hand each aspect of our lives over to Him. Practically this is not always easy. We get caught in a busy day and God just seems to drop off the agenda.

In our daily lives, there need to be moments devoted to Him. Moments when everything else stops. Moments when the focus shifts off us and onto Him. Moments when we realize that He's been waiting there all along. Moments when reality kicks in.

So much of our time as Christians is spent looking at the issues we face and the difficulties that we have to overcome. We need to learn to focus more upon Him and less upon the impossibilities and the hardships. When we spend too much time looking at where we are rather than where we're headed, the focus shifts and our faith gets disheartened. The writer of Psalm 73 was living under the notion that 'the grass is greener on the other side'. Then God catches his eye and he realizes that he has salvation. When we truly focus upon Him, our priorities fall into place.

How many times a day do we stop and re-focus?

Let's take more opportunities to redirect our focus – lift our eyes up out of the world and focus on God. Let's get lost in His awe and wonder – even when we are sat behind the computer screen. Most importantly, let's remind ourselves of why we are thankful.

For me, my walk with Christ is punctuated with holy moments when I suddenly remember what life is all about. They come at the most bizarre times, when I'm waiting for the kettle to boil or as I sit at a red light. There are certain times that are so intense that everything else in the world seems to disappear and it is as if I am face-to-face with Jesus and that is all that matters.

People often ask me, if God is this great big God, why does He need our pathetic thanks? Why should He care?

I believe that we often fail to understand the impact that worshipping God has upon us. Worshipping God helps us to recognize where the good things come from. In the Western world we live with such abundance and still complain! Every day God gives us so much and we take it for granted. For many Christians, our walk with God is about putting forward requests and then forgetting to thank Him for what He has done in response.

We need to spend time reflecting upon the great gifts that God gives us. Our lives of worship help us to recognize our own limitations and how much more we need to rely upon Him. As we begin to thank Him for what He has done, we are brought back to the cross. As our understanding of the cross increases, surely our desire to give thanks will grow, too.

Worship – what's ya problem?

It is not always easy living a life of worship. As a generation, many of us run on emotions. Discipline is an alien term banished from our discipleship. We like to go with the flow. In my life there are times when I want to worship God – when I am so stoked on who He is and what He has done for me that it just happens. Yet there are other times when I am not in that place – times when I am tired and, to be blunt, can't be bothered. Sometimes it happens when life is good. I float on autopilot, feeling satisfied with life and my walk with God. At other times, it is when life gets tough and I get distracted by the world around.

> Worship is defined as 'All that we are, responding to all that God is'.
>
> John Drane, *Faith in a Changing Culture*
> (Zondervan, 1997)

But it is important that worship becomes a discipline – giving over each day to God as it comes. For a number of

months the welcome note on my phone stated 'My heart
will choose to say'. I first heard the song 'Blessed be Your
Name' during a Sunday morning service, and my heart
wept. There was something about the poetry of that song
that resonated with me. I realized that no matter how bad
things got down here God was still worthy of praise up
there. At the time life was pretty good but over the next few
months my life started to go down the drain. Throughout
that time I had a daily choice to make. Do I stop giving God
the praise He's due or do I recognize that in everything,
good and bad, His name is worthy to be praised?

> Sometimes we go through trials and testing for that
> very reason, because the God who loves us wants us
> to rely on him more completely or to trust him more
> fully.
>
> David Jackman, *The Message of John's Letters*
> (InterVarsity Press, 1992)

I have learnt to know that God is always with me,
holding me by the hand, guiding me where I should go.
Though everything might be going wrong for me down
here, all I want and all I could ever desire is Him.

That does not mean that we have to get caught up
in 'Nice Christianity' where everything is about hiding
behind a façade of smiles. Sometimes I need to sit down
and weep. No words. No clichés. No joy. No jumping up
and down. Sometimes it's necessary to walk up to Jesus
and cry out 'WHY?!?' But is that being any less worshipful?
'Careful,' I'm told, 'Don't treat God with disrespect.' Yet
David, honoured by God as a man after His own heart,
was unafraid to repeatedly turn round to God and yell
'What are you playing at?!'

Worship is not about lying and saying everything is hunky-dory when it blatantly isn't. Nor is it about saying 'But that's OK God'. It is, however, about saying 'You're God and I'm not. I will worship you – but this is where I'm at and this is where I meet you today.' I was in a worship service recently and the songs were soft and sappy – all about how great God was ... I had to leave the church for a few minutes and worship God with shouting and running outside so that I could be real with how I was doing in my walk with Him. Celebrating God's love but in a more unruly manner!

Worship – kickin' off

The gift of creativity gives us a way of reflecting on our walk with God – even if we don't see ourselves as particularly creative. We need to rediscover the creative arts. In such a materialistic society we tend to buy in all of our worship music rather than writing songs that reflect where we are as a local church. Maybe some of us have suffered tremendously and we need to have the opportunity to respond to God with laments like Jeremiah did. God wants us to worship Him in freedom. Painting and sculpture, dance and drama – use the arts as expressions of worship to God. Just go wild and dance foolishly in worship!

David knew how to worship. In 2 Samuel he worshipped in wild abandonment when the ark returned to Jerusalem – he stripped and danced for the Lord. What makes it so amazing is that David was no child, he was king of one of the most powerful nations on earth. Can you imagine the president of the USA publicly worshipping in such a fashion?

If David was able to worship in such a way, what stops us from going crazy and allowing our praise to manifest itself in such ways? David's wife was pretty miffed when she saw him – embarrassed by the spectacle. Lives of worship affect those around – they cause reactions. Perhaps we are too afraid to worship in the liberty that God wants for us because of the fear of humiliation. Is this the source of our monochrome worship.

> Satan's ploy has been to keep us so full of junk that we're not hungry for Him, and it has worked magnificently for centuries. The enemy has made us so accustomed to surviving on an earthly prosperity but a beggar subsistence in the spirit realm, that just a crumb of God's presence will satisfy. There are those who are not content with crumbs anymore. They want HIM and nothing else will do. A full loaf! Counterfeits no longer satisfy or interest them; they must have the REAL THING. Most of us, however, keep our lives so jammed with junk food for the soul and amusements for the flesh that we don't know what it is to be really hungry.
>
> Tommy Tenney, *The God Chasers* (STL, 1999)

I frequently find myself in humiliating situations. As a surfer, I am always wave hungry! Many surfers dedicate their lives to surfing and at university I would go to extraordinary lengths to score good waves. I would often feel quite foolish as farmers watched me jog with my surfboard past their sheep. Especially when it was 7 a.m. and the fields were coated with snow! It was all done in the search for perfect waves. It is quite scary some of the lengths people go in their search of waves. Over my travels I have met people who have sacrificed education, careers and families in pursuit of big clean swells.

What are you really passionate about? What do you daydream about? When you look at the last week and calculate where your money and time has been spent, it often shows you what you are passionate for.

Worship is also about hungering for more of God. In his book *The God Chasers*, Tommy Tenney shares a great picture of God the Father. He tells a story of a young child trying to catch his father. The child keeps lunging to grasp the father but the father easily manoeuvres away each time. Eventually, the father's heart is touched. He sees how much the child wants to be with him and is overcome with a desire to be with the child. He swoops down, picks up and embraces the child.

As a child I know that I can never catch God. However, I capture His heart as I chase after Him. He watches and sees how much I desire to be with Him. I love that promise in Matthew that as we seek Him, we will find Him. He is obedient to that promise and meets with me. Our worship reflects our heart and our desire to be with Him. How much do we seek after God in our worship?

Worshipping God is not about what He needs. It's about our relationship with Him. It's about recognizing all that God deserves. And when we make time for Him, when we put Him first, He meets us. He's waiting for you now.

Relax your body . . .
Open your mind . . .
Engage your spirit . . .
This is the house of God
Prepare to worship.

Life is an indescribable gift
Our worship is a celebration of that gift
And of the giver
In our worship we have rediscovered
God's marvellous affirmation of life.

This is different from the faith
That many of us experienced in the past
Religion that was life-denying
Worship that was monochrome and one-
    dimensional
Where our senses were left at the door.

Tonight we invite you to bring all that you are into
    worship
Your struggles and your failures
Your joys and fears,
Your faith and your doubts.
Your culture
Your sensuality
Your whole self

Bring your self and be at home now
God is here
And all are welcome.

Jonny Baker, Doug Gay and Jenny Brown,
Alternative Worship (Baker Books, 2004)

RECAP

Worship is about getting perspective

Worship is about the heart

Worship is about giving thanks

Worship is about chasing after God

Worship is about relationship

Getting practical

- Go through the Alphabet from A to Z and think of a name that you could give God for every letter. For example, A could be Almighty ... Put the list somewhere that you will often see it so that you can reflect on the many characteristics of the God we serve.

- Slow down. Next time you take a journey, leave earlier and spend time watching the environment around you. Can you see aspects of God in your environment? When you see something of Him, stop, reflect and recognize.

- Take opportunities to be alone in creation – spend time listening to the sounds around you. Concentrate on your breathing. Breathe in God and breathe out pride.

- How are you comfortable worshipping God? How can you be more risky in your daily worship? Push the boundaries of what you are willing to do. For example, spend time shouting out your praise (perhaps not on the High Street!).

- Spend some time reflecting on the cross. Draw or make a cross and write on it several related verses. Use a concordance to help you scan the New Testament for relevant verses.

- Accountability partners. To make sure repentance is more than just lip-service, find accountability partners. It's always cool to get mates that you can really trust and to be honest with over areas in which you are struggling. You could even have a hot seat, when your mates can ask you anything about your walk with God.

- Written confession. Spend time waiting upon God, allowing Him to pinpoint areas of your life that are not right. Jot them down and spend time doing business with God – working out how you can change and then allowing God's Spirit to equip you. You might want to burn the list afterwards as a sign that it is past and that you have a new beginning!

- Think about how you use your money – would Jesus use it in the same way? Discuss with friends about the issue of tithing – should we tithe today?

- Communion is a great way of remembering what Christ has done – it is a powerful experience. Why not take time out to break bread with a mate or by yourself. Read 1 Corinthians 11 while you spend time focusing upon God.

- Soak in God! Lie on your bed and listen to some chill-out music giving thanks for all the good stuff that God gives you. Spend time just being in His presence.

- Pilgrimage. Go on a journey of worship to a sacred place – a church, monastery or cross. As you walk reflect upon your life as a journey and reflect on how you have lived out daily worship over the years. How can you live a more fruitful life of worship?

- Put a slogan right by your bed that will remind you to live a life of worship each day. As you read it pray that the Spirit will equip you to live out a life of worship in the activities of the day.

- Make an effort to make the most of your senses. Enjoy the taste of food and touch of different items of furniture. Too often we fail to appreciate the little things in life.

- Read a psalm out loud. Repeat it several times and then start paraphrasing it in your own words. As you do so, you might even want to start singing it aloud.

- Write songs and poetry that honestly reflect your situation with God.

- Pop on the hi-fi and dance! Cheesy but I bet God loves it!

- Rediscover the use of candles. Light them one at a time whilst reading John 1. Give thanks for the light that Jesus makes in your life.

- Root out some church liturgy from previous centuries and re-discover how people worshipped in previous generations. What do those words mean for us today?

- Read the passage John 4:23–24 and meditate on what it means to worship in spirit and truth.

- Get hold of some clay and mould an image that represents your worship to God.

Further reading

To get started ...

For the Audience of One, Mike Pilavachi and Craig Borlase, Hodder & Stoughton Religious, 1999

The Unquenchable Worshipper, Matt Redman, Kingsway Communications, 2001

In depth ...

Alternative Worship, Jonny Baker, Doug Gay and Jenny Brown, Baker Books, 2004

Facedown, Matt Redman, Louie Giglio, Regal books, 2004

In Pursuit of God, A.W. Tozer, Christian Publications, 1982

True Worship, Vaughan Roberts, Paternoster Lifestyle, 2002

A Heart For Worship, Graham Kendrick, Hodder & Stoughton Religious, 1995

like a child
to see You thru innocent eyes
nothing to cloud
pure faith
revert me
simple and true
He loves me
forget the intellectual
put away the knowledge
grace sweep me off my feet
to lay facedown at Yours
awe and wonder
at your power
majestic perfection
my sin humbles me
i realize Your affection
He loves me.

MARCY BURNHAM

4

let's talk

jo wells

So there I was, in Brazil, all alone, waiting to be met
by a Brazilian mission team. Only one problem – no-
one on the team spoke fluent English and languages
are not my strong point. I was to be doing mission
without English for ten days. How was this going to
work? I did all of the normal things that a Brit does
when there is a translation issue. I started by speaking
really slowly. When that didn't work, I started putting
on a funky accent because that always helps!

As the mission progressed I understood that they
were asking me to preach one night and that they
would find me a translator. I had only preached
a couple of sermons before but I was up for the
challenge. The opportunity to chat in English to
a translator who would understand me sounded
especially good! And if it all went pear-shaped, I
would soon be leaving the country. I explained my
lack of experience but they still seemed keen. I was
to preach the following night.

That afternoon, I was wandering around the streets
of the city with the team looking for somewhere to
eat. Now, in Brazil they have these cars that drive
around the streets with PA systems strapped onto the
roof announcing big events. One of these cars kept

driving along the row of shops, blasting out some advert. As it drove past again and again, it sounded like my name was erupting from the speakers in a flurry of Portuguese. 'It couldn't be,' I thought, though it did sound very familiar. I decided to risk confusion and ask what the message on the antennae was actually advertising.

One of the team turned to me and explained that it was in fact an advert for me! The local church was so pleased to have me speaking that they had hired these vehicles to announce that the international evangelist from the United Kingdom was here to preach. The *international evangelist* from the UK?! What happened to the fact that I had only preached twice before? More than that, he explained that it was a new church building opening event! This was going to be far bigger than I had imagined, and far more than I could handle! What had I got myself into?

Andy Frost

When communication breaks down, you can often get yourself into crazy situations. Communication is the key to relationship. When it goes wrong it leads to all kinds of misunderstanding. Prayer is simply about communicating with God. It is the most essential part of our relationship with Him, but too often it's the first thing to slip.

It's all about relationship

Jesus had an amazing relationship with God the Father. Time after time He proclaimed the richness and intensity of the relationship they shared. John 8:26, 28–29 says '. . . he who sent me is reliable, and what I heard from him I tell the world . . . I do nothing on my own, but speak just what the Father has taught me. The one who sent me is with me; he has not left me alone.' Luke tells us that Jesus often sought a lonely place to pray. The communion Jesus experienced with the Father was so intimate that He stated 'The Father and I are one' (Jn. 10:30). At the cross that relationship was ripped apart as Jesus actually became sin for us (2 Cor. 5:21). Moments before He died He cried to His Father, 'My God why have you forsaken me.' (Mt. 27:46). Communion with God had stopped and Jesus knew it immediately.

I'm not very good at remembering to charge my phone. It's not exactly unheard of for me to be chatting away and realize that I have been talking to a piece of plastic for the past few minutes without noticing that my battery has died. Feeling fairly embarrassed I quickly stuff my phone in my pocket and hope that no-one around me has realized that I have been talking to myself! Often I can go hours without even thinking about God, a whole day without fixing my attention solely on Him. If the presence of God were to leave me, it would probably take me an age for it to dawn on me that He had gone.

We all have access to the most privileged relationship in the world, a relationship with our Creator. Yet we don't always take advantage of that fact. In the height of busyness, stress and fast-paced lifestyles, our prayer life is often the first thing to go. John Wesley understood the purpose of prayer. He would get up every day to pray for 2 hours from 5 a.m. till 7 a.m. If he had a busy day ahead, he wouldn't skip it, instead he would get up at four! We are told that when He was tired, Jesus would go and pray instead of going for a quick nap. That's where His strength and His compassion for people came from. God is waiting for you to let Him be God in the situations you find yourself in. Chase after Him in prayer and He promises that you will find Him.

> Whether we like it or not, asking is the rule of the Kingdom. If you may have everything by asking His Name, and nothing without asking, I beg you to see how absolutely vital prayer is.
>
> Charles Spurgeon, from 'Ask and Have', a sermon on James 4:2–3, delivered on 1 October 1882; *Metropolitan Tabernacle Pulpit* Volume 28

I had just got back from two months in South America on mission and I was tired. Lying on my bed I was enjoying the opportunity to simply chat to God, it felt like the first time in ages that we'd had the chance to catch up and ask each other, 'How you doing?'

This prayer session took me to a place of God's presence that I don't think I'd ever been to before. I was right there in the 'sanctuary' talking to God, my Dad, about all the stupid things that swim around in my head. It was two weeks before the start of my final year at university, so my main focus was the future. 'Where am I going Daddy? What have you got planned for me? My husband, Daddy, how's he doing today? Do I know him yet? What about my kids, are you looking after them for me? Will you look after them when I mess up or let them down?' I started thinking about being pregnant with these kids I was praying for – me with a big belly and stretch marks. 'O God! Am I going to have swollen ankles when I'm pregnant?'

I was in the throne room of The Holy God Most High, and all I could hear was laughter ringing in my ears. I had the most direct access to the Author and Perfecter of everything, able to ask Him anything – and the question in my head was not about world poverty or the mystery of the Trinity, but whether I am going to get swollen ankles when I'm pregnant! The delight I could feel from God because of that question still makes me giggle today.

Prayer is not about the right phrases or how many Bible quotes you can include. It's about sitting down with Daddy and catching up with Him. He wants you. He wants you to sit on His knee. From there you can share your heart with Him and capture His heart for you. From there comes the inspiration to live a life that honours Daddy. You know Him, you know what it takes to make Him proud. But you also know that when you don't cut it, when you don't make the grade – all He wants is for you to come and sit back on His knee, so He can wipe away the tears, give you a hug and whisper in your ear, 'I love you. I love you. I love you.'

I look at those around me, and I see that so many have no concept of someone whispering 'I love you' in their ears. Somewhere in our lives we get broken. We all have a moment when we were told we were never going to be good enough. That we are not going to make the grade. We live our lives in the knowledge that we have failed to live up to expectations, we suffer guilt knowing that we've let someone down.

Part of our communication with God is about allowing Him to heal that wound, allowing Him to show us that He didn't make a mistake when He made us, that He loves us just as we are. He wants us to have the right relationship with Him as our Father, our Heavenly Father. A relationship where the things we have longed for in our relationships are fulfilled in Him. I know many people who struggle with the fatherhood of God. I know I did. But I do have a perfect image of what I wanted from my dad, even if I don't necessarily get it. I know what that relationship could have looked like. And I know that God offers me exactly that picture. My biggest issue now is that of trust. I know the ideal. The picture-perfect Father–child relationship. I also know how impossible it is to achieve. Part of me is just waiting for God to let me down.

Honesty

There have been times in my life where I have taken myself away from the world around me because I need to scream my anger out at God. The disappointments I have felt in my life have been acute, and have often been events that occurred in direct contradiction to what I had felt God had been saying to me. Who do you go to when you can't go to God? What do you do when you can't trust your Heavenly Father any more than your earthly one? The only answer I could find was in John 6:68. People were leaving Jesus because His teaching was too hard for them to take. He challenges the disciples asking if they are going to leave Him, too. But Peter replies, '... to whom shall we go? You have the words of eternal life.' I have felt as if God has let me down. But it could only be God to whom I could voice my disappointments.

Job accused God of inflicting all that was going against Him, and God didn't deny any of it. Even though we, the readers, know that Satan was the perpetrator of it all (Job 1:12), God simply said He would be God (Job 41:11). Yet He praised Job, for speaking what was right before Him. Job's accusations were finally silenced when he saw the Living Lord (Job 42:5). He knew the holiness in Him and could not pass judgement on the Lord Himself.

God's name is Faithful Father. The situations I find myself in aren't always what I desire for myself. But when every inch of me wants to run away from God, I will remain and pray. I will trust Him and allow Him to heal me, because Daddy really does know best. Life often throws us things that we don't understand, makes us question what we're doing and what exactly it is that we're following. But the question isn't 'what?' it's 'who?'. Keeping the lines of communication open is the most important thing. Keep seeking after God, He is faithful and will be faithful even when you can't see how.

The stop gap

Give yourself no rest and give God no rest until He establishes His kingdom (Is. 62:6–7). Abraham had the audacity to ask God to change His mind over the destruction of Sodom and Gomorrah. Moses pleaded for mercy over the Israelites and God relented. God listens to the cries of His people. Indeed God searches the land looking for one righteous person who will stand in the gap between Him and the people (Ezek. 22:30). Whenever I read that I feel convicted. Would I be sufficient? Could I, with the life that I live, stand in front of God on behalf of others?

You must pray with all your might. That does not mean saying your prayers, or sitting gazing about in church or chapel with eyes wide open while someone else says them for you. It means fervent, effectual, untiring wrestling with God. This kind of prayer be sure the devil and the world and your indolent, unbelieving nature will oppose. They will pour water on this flame.

William Booth, his last public address
given on 9 May 1912,
www.stpetersnottingham.org/heroes/booth.htm

This is the call of the intercessor. To plead for God's mercy rather than His judgement. Our prayers start with our relationship with God, but they cannot stop there. We need to be praying for others. Once we recognize the power of God as King over our own lives – we surely must be moved to beg that God brings others into the same position.

How much do you want God to be God in your life? In your family situation? In your town? In your church? In your friends' lives? In work or school or college?

Do you want Him to be God enough to yell at Him, to hassle Him for the sake of those you love?

Jacob was a guy who was prepared to risk anything for what he wanted. One night in the loneliest place he could find, he met with God. And wrestled Him to the floor (Gen. 32).

'Bless me!' he cried. 'I won't let go till you bless me.' Jacob was a big guy. He had worked the land for years. Strong and tough, he could handle most things. But wrestling God must be like trying to wrestle a hurricane. Impossible. How much it must have hurt, and yet he clung on. Through gritted teeth he cried 'Bless me!' God dislocated his hip and still he clung on. All through the night a man wrestled with God. And at daybreak God left, blessing him.

When would you let go? When would you turn round and say 'Oh that must not be God's will?' If you want God to be active in your life and in the lives of those around you pray to Him with persistence. He respects it. He demands it. Be cheeky. Don't leave God's presence without being satisfied, whatever it takes, stick it out. Trust me – trust Jesus, (check out Lk. 18, Jn. 15 and Mt. 6 – it's all there!). It'll be worth it in the end.

Intercession is often coupled with spiritual warfare. Daniel 10:2–14 tells us of how Daniel was praying to God for three weeks, fasting and mourning all that time. On the twenty-fourth day, Daniel had a vision of someone that looked like a man, who came in answer to his prayers. Daniel had been heard and answered the moment he started praying, yet it took three weeks before the answer reached him. Why? Because there was a spiritual battle happening at the same time. Sometimes we don't even know that we are in a battle, but our prayers affect far more than we often give them credit for. God moves when we pray.

More than words

You walk in, a silence hits you that you recognize. A tangible silence that signals God is here. You glance at the walls and see colour flowing across the room. People's hearts have been graffitied in paint, calling out to God as individuals with one voice, for God to come and be among us.

> Love us
> Heal us
> Guide us
> Restore us

The passion with which people pray is displayed for all to see. Not for recognition but because they could not express their prayers in any other way.

You walk across the floor. Avoiding the glass and bread. You read the words 'Broken for you' and look up to a mural of the cross stretched over windows. In the corner is a single candle flickering in the air – the light came into the darkness and the darkness has not overcome it. Your mind wanders to a place of fear, where Jesus might have failed, yet there is comfort. You remember He lives. A silent sense of thanks escapes you.

Surrounding you are newspapers showing war, poverty, need and apathy. 'Only God can save this,' you think, 'God fix this, please.'

You pick up a piece of clay. The potter's hand that moulds us, breaks us and shapes us. 'I place my life in your hands' you think as you form the clay into a tiny representation of yourself.

Prayer rooms have been popping up all over the place in the last few years. Quite simply they are a place where you can pray. God is with us all the time, but sometimes it's helpful to use space and creativity to express the different ways we can pray.

But we don't have to be in a designated room to pray creatively. Take a walk around your neighbourhood. What do you see? How can your surroundings help focus your attention, your thoughts and prayers?

Prayer isn't just about words, it's about opening our-selves up in relationship to God. Different tools can be used to aid us in our communication with God. Arts or meditation, reading or sculpting, just as they can help us express our worship to God they can also allow us to craft and concentrate our prayers to Him. Lift up your hearts. Connect with God in whatever way you can express yourself. He has made you unique, find a way you pray which suits who you are in Christ.

> . . . pray in the Spirit on all occasions with all kinds of prayers and requests . . .
>
> **Ephesians 6:18**

I remember attending my first charismatic church meeting. The people there prayed differently to what I was used to growing up. They spoke in weird languages, and they suggested things that they felt God was saying to individuals in the meeting. They lifted their hands up in prayer. People were praying for others in the congregation, asking God for healing and information about their situation. They kept saying that they were desperate for God to move. It was weird. Although I could tell that Jesus was the focus of the meeting, things that happened there were completely outside of my experience.

Sometimes we get scared of the unknown. We don't always understand what makes people pray in ways other than the ones we feel comfortable with. Fear can keep us from encountering God in a new way. It's sometimes easier to say that it's wrong than it is to find out what's actually going on and experience something new.

Charismatic prayer quite simply means prayer in tune with the Holy Spirit. I don't believe that God has left us to our own devices. Jesus died so that His Helper could come. Jesus hasn't returned, so our Helper is still here. The Holy Spirit doesn't just move within the Bible, He is living and active today. If prayer is foundational to our relationship with God, then the Holy Spirit must be foundational in our prayers. The problem is when we open ourselves up to God's way of doings things, things can get a little interesting. In 1 Corinthians 12–14, Paul commands us to seek spiritual gifts, not to be afraid of them. He teaches us how to use them with respect to those around us, without letting things get out of control. But he stresses the importance of spiritual gifts to our relationship with God and the impact the gifts can have on others.

Moving in the prophetic

As we discussed in chapter 3, God is a Holy God and we enter His presence with reverence and with boldness. The attitude of worship should be found in every prayer that we utter to God. Just like worship, prayer is a two-way thing. Us talking to God and God speaking back.

Elijah was a mighty prophet, defeating the counterfeit religions and bringing God's word to kings and commoners alike. But he was afraid. The queen had killed all the prophets of the Lord, Elijah was the last one left and now she was after him, too. So he sought after God in prayer on a mountaintop. The word of God came to him and told him to get ready because the presence of the Lord was coming.

Huddled in a cave, Elijah waited for the Lord to appear. A great wind tore the mountain apart but the Lord was not in it and Elijah remained where he was. Next, an earthquake shook the ground, but God wasn't there either. Then there was a fire, but no God. Finally there came a gentle whisper, and Elijah knew it was the Lord (1 Kgs. 19:1–18). As Christians, we often expect God to speak to us in the mighty and the dramatic and forget to listen for that gentle whisper.

Elijah had seen God move in some pretty powerful ways, he knew His might and power. But he could also recognize God in the still small voice. He knew the variety of ways that the Lord speaks and recognized Him in all of them.

Jesus said that His sheep would know His voice. We are the sheep and Jesus wants to speak to us. Jesus says 'He who belongs to God hears what God says ...' (Jn. 8:47).

The first time I heard the idea that God speaks to us today – I laughed! Silly idea! But when I thought about it, I realized that God had spoken to people all through the Bible, so why should He suddenly shut up today?

The truth is that we have all heard God speak. Maybe not the big booming 'voice of God' that you might find in the movies. But by the very fact you are a Christian you have responded to God calling you home.

Problem is that we often don't believe that God would bother to speak to 'little me'. Big holy prophets get to hear God. Anointed preachers on the big stage might even get to hear God. Nuns shut away in some Italian mountain might hear God, but not you, not me.

Gideon was an insignificant man. His family was the down and out of the neighbourhood, and he was the youngest, most inferior member of his family. If anyone could be sure that God was *not* going to speak to them, it was Gideon. But God did speak and he called Gideon to lead the nation of Israel in battle (Judg. 6). God has always had a heart for the unlikely people, the insignificant, the 'nothing special.' He created us, planned us, and chose us, why would He not want to speak to us? There isn't a special holy type of person that is capable of hearing God, we all hear Him in different ways, from a loud audible voice, to simple intuition. We can know how God speaks to us, when we allow Him to.

Maybe we feel as if we shouldn't bother God with our little issues. After all He is God and does have rather a lot to do! We'll handle this one and turn to God when it's really important. We shouldn't take up too much of His time. But Jesus tells us to pray to God about even our daily bread (Lk. 11:3). The most basic of food and God provides it. Jesus tells us not to worry about our clothes or our homes because God sustains them all (Mt. 6:25–34). God is totally concerned with the little things.

Maybe God has never stopped talking, maybe it's just that we've stopped listening?

Where are our priorities? Do we stop long enough and allow God to speak, into our situations, into the lives of those around us? Do we practise quietening ourselves enough so that we are 'tuned in' to what God wants to say to us?

We need to learn to settle our own thoughts down, so that we focus on God rather than ourselves in our prayers, then ask God to speak. It's a simple thing but we often forget it.

A Native American and his friend were down town in New York City near Times Square. It was during the noon hour and the streets were filled with people. Cars were honking their horns, taxicabs were squealing round corners, sirens were wailing, the sounds of the city were almost deafening. Suddenly the Native American said 'I hear a cricket.' His friend said, 'What? You must be crazy. You can't possibly hear a cricket in all this noise!'

'No, I'm sure of it! I hear a cricket' the Native replied.

The Native American listened carefully for a moment, walked across the street to a big cement planter where some shrubs were growing. He looked into the bushes, beneath the branches and sure enough he located a small cricket. His friend was utterly amazed.

'That's incredible', said his friend. 'You must have superhuman hearing!'

'No,' said the Native, 'My ears are no different from yours; it all depends on what you are listening for.'
'But it can't be!' said his friend, 'I could never hear a cricket in all this noise'.

'Yes it's true' came the reply, 'It depends on what is really important to you. Here, let me show you what I mean.'

He reached into his pocket, pulled out a few coins, and discreetly dropped them on the sidewalk. And then, with the noise of the crowded street still blaring in their ears, they noticed every head within 20 feet turn and look to see if the money that tinkled on the pavement was theirs.

'See what I mean?' asked the Native, ' It all depends on what's important to you.'

Author unknown from *Notes on Listening to God*,
Donna Jordan

God might show you a picture or suggest a Bible verse to read. He might give you a sense of something, a feeling, a word or sentence. He might speak to you in a conversation or through a dream. What about asking God to speak through a film or the book you're reading? Looking at a piece of art? Like with Elijah, we need to be expectant that God will speak, but open as to how He will do it.

I was travelling home on the train one day minding my own business, when I spotted out of the corner of my eye a lady slumped over on her seat crying quietly to herself, oblivious to those around her. As I watched her, I asked God why she was so upset. I asked God to tell me what had happened to her that had made her so utterly miserable?

In my mind I heard 'Sing O barren women'.

Yeah right that was God! What a cliché! You see a woman in her twenties and you automatically think 'man trouble' or 'kids'.

'That's not God that's just me,' I thought to myself. But the voice continued 'you who never bore a child ... your descendants will cover the earth.' (Isaiah 54)

'Come on God,' I thought to myself, 'give me something I can work with here.' I didn't dare share those words with her – I could have been completely wrong and then what would she have thought?! I could have ended up looking really stupid.

But I couldn't ignore the prompting and as we both stood up to get off the train, I asked her if she was alright. 'Tell her what I've said,' I heard God say.

'No,' I replied, 'let's see what she says first.'

She looked up at me through her thick eye make-up and matted hair, and sighed. 'He dumped me,' she said. 'I can't have kids and he dumped me.'

I couldn't believe it! I had heard God right and missed my opportunity. I walked home kicking myself. God had spoken, I had heard Him and yet I had done nothing for fear of embarrassment.

Although we might be happy to go along with the idea that God will speak to us. It's harder to trust when it's God talking to us about other people. When God speaks, it's often easy to ignore Him, thinking it's just us, or that we're imagining things. But God has always spoken to people, calling them out of their tiny concept of the world, into a mind-blowing relationship with Him. He asks us to be His mouthpieces.

Fear stops us from asking for the gift of prophecy, and fear certainly stops many of us from using it. But God charges us: 'Do not put out the Spirit's fire; do not treat prophecies with contempt. Test everything. Hold on to the good. Avoid every kind of evil.' (1 Thess. 5:19–21). Therefore if we are worried that we might be speaking our own words despite our best intentions, God doesn't want us to be afraid. 'Try it out,' He says, if you're wrong just discard it. Ask others with discernment and see what is of God and what isn't. If you are right then it will be all good! Paul commands us to eagerly ask God for the gift of prophecy (1 Cor. 14:1). Let's not pass up on the opportunity to witness God speaking to others through us.

Gobbledegook

The gift of tongues portrayed in Acts gives witness to an outpouring of the Holy Spirit. When people accepted Jesus and what He did on the cross, the Spirit filled them and they began praising God in different languages – otherwise known as 'tongues'.

Some people credit the gift of tongues as a physical sign that someone has been filled with the Holy Spirit. But the Bible isn't explicit on this issue. What it does say is that a person praying in tongues is encouraged and developed.

Often we don't have a clue what we are saying or why, but allowing the Holy Spirit to take control in our prayers can only be a good thing.

I prayed for years for the gift of tongues and didn't receive one single syllable. I thought there was something wrong with me as a Christian. That I wasn't holy enough to get the gift. It wasn't until I came to an understanding that it was God's gift to give not mine to demand that I was patient enough to receive it and be able to pray in tongues.

Even then I didn't fully trust it. When I was little I used to speak in pretend languages (mainly to annoy my sister!) and this felt really similar. Was it all just gobbledegook? But then why could I only say one sentence over and over again? Then someone explained to me. When a child learns its first word, 'Dada', everything gets called Dada: the chair, the table, 'change my nappy', whatever. As the child's language skills develop so too does her or his vocabulary and the child will start using more and more words.

Likewise with tongues. When we start out we tend to only say a few words – the more we use the gift the more proficient in it we become.

> The one concern of the devil is to keep Christians from praying. He fears nothing from prayerless studies, prayerless work, and prayerless religion. He laughs at our toil, mocks at our wisdom, but trembles when we pray.
>
> Anonymous (www.justpray.net)

The gifts of the Spirit are always given to give glory back to God. Peter rebuked Simon the Sorcerer for thinking that he could gain personally with the gift of the Holy Spirit

(Acts 8:9–24). We need to keep our intentions in check when asking for and using spiritual gifts. But nevertheless, the power of prayer when the Holy Spirit is involved is indeed a powerful and awesome thing!

Going without to get more

> Prayer is reaching out after the unseen; fasting is letting go of all that is seen and temporal. Fasting helps express, deepen, confirm the resolution that we are ready to sacrifice anything, even ourselves to attain what we seek for the kingdom of God.
>
> **Andrew Murray, *With Christ in the School of Prayer*** **(Ambassador Publications, 1998)**

Denying ourselves of something important to us puts our priorities into perspective. On the simplest level, fasting is all about reminding ourselves and showing God how important something is to us. The reprimand the people received in Isaiah 58 is because their actions didn't match their prayers. Without necessarily fully understanding the spiritual significance of fasting, we are clearly told throughout the Bible that we should fast as an act of repentance. It is an act of acknowledgement of returning God to His rightful place at the top of our priorities. From there God is able to be fully God in our lives.

> No revival in history has ever just happened! Prayer always precedes a great move of God.
>
> **John Kilpatrick, *Feast of Fire* (Zondervan, 1997)**

'If my people, who are called by my name, will humble themselves and pray and seek my face and turn from their wicked ways, then will I hear from heaven and will forgive their sin and will heal their land.' (2 Chr. 7:14). There is a humbling aspect inherent in prayer. Like fasting, when we pray we acknowledge that we are nothing without God.

A few months ago, I got quite ill and ended up in hospital on copious amounts of painkillers. I was so frustrated. I could barely move, let alone do anything. I couldn't even take a shower! I hated it. People had to care for me. I couldn't take care of myself. People joked around saying that it was God teaching me a lesson. Well why couldn't He teach me a lesson by sending me on a free holiday to the Bahamas? Why do all of God's lessons have to be quite so painful? But God had to get my attention somehow. The point was I had become too independent. Depending on my own strength instead of listening to and depending on God. Self-sufficiency is the opposite of God's desire for us. He wants us to recognize Him as sovereign over all situations.

Marie Monsen was a revivalist in China during the 1930s and 40s. She toured churches around China, convicting people of their sin and calling them into a right relationship with Jesus. C.L. Culpepper was a Baptist minister. For four years he led his church in prayer as they sought after God, crying out on their knees. After four years Marie Monsen turned to C.L. Culpepper and declared; 'God must come, you've fulfilled the requirements.' And boy did He come! The revival at Shantung lasted fifteen years.

When God is in His rightful place, He moves. I desperately want to see God move in the UK and around the world. I want to see God worshipped by my friends and my family. I want to see the promises in the Bible fulfilled in my lifetime. God can do it! Revival can happen. And it all starts with prayer.

RECAP

Prayer is about talking to God,

Prayer is about listening to God

Prayer is about standing in the gap

Prayer is about perseverance

Prayer is about transformation

Practical tips

- Try turning your wardrobe into your very own prayer room. Put photos of your family on the doors and include a map of the world, newspaper articles, Bible verses and sand in the wardrobe bottom, with paper, pens and modelling clay. When you're getting ready in the mornings, enter a holy space in your bedroom!

- Sometimes it's easier or helpful to write a letter of prayer to God. Tell Him how you feel, what's going on in your life.

- Find a friend and wrestle each other, crying out to God to act.

- Read Luke 11:1–4. Why do you think the disciples wanted Jesus to teach them how to pray? What lessons can you learn from His answer?

- Paint or sculpt your prayers, creating a physical representation of how you feel, or what you want to do.

- Try praying using musical instruments and follow beats and rhythms on a drum or bongos or just the side of your desk.

- Go on a walk with God. Pray about what you see, calm your thoughts and stop at certain landmarks and ask God to speak back.

- Always in a rush? Why don't you choose the longer route in the morning, or pick the longest queue in the shop. While you're waiting – pray.

- Create a photograph box of the people you want to pray for. As you go through the pictures each day pray for the individuals

- Read local and national newspapers and ask God to move in the situations you read about.

- Get a map of the world – and pray over a different country each day. Find out what's happening there if you can and ask God to bless that nation.

- Write to your local council/police/school asking them if they have any prayer requests. Or even put up a prayer box in public places asking if people would like prayer about certain issues.

- Read Luke 10:38–42. Which character do you identify most with? What do you think Jesus wants you to spend more time doing?

- Why don't you and some friends become secret prayer angels. Put all your names in a hat, pull out one each and commit to praying for that person every day.

- Write a list of the people you would like to know Jesus. Pray over that list every day.

- Why not get a Christian pen pal from a different country? Find out about their struggles in their country and tell them about yours. Pray for each other on-line, in letters or on the phone.

- Why don't you host a 24–7 prayer week or even just a weekend? Find a room and you and some mates commit to manning it the whole time it's open with prayer, divided up into hour-long slots.

Further reading

To get started ...

Red Moon Rising, Pete Greig and Dave Roberts, Kingsway, 2004

Notes on Listening to God, Donna Jordan, 1999

How Not to Pray, Jeff Lucas, Authentic Lifestyle, 2003

In depth ...

Too Busy Not to Pray, Bill Hybels, InterVarsity Press, 2001

Intercessory Prayer, Dutch Sheets, Gospel Light, 1997

A Call to Spiritual Reformation: Priorities from Paul and His Prayers, D.A. Carson, InterVarsity Press, 1992

Awakening Cry, Pete Greig, Silver Fish Publishing, 1998

My eloquence has no relevance in your presence.
Forget eloquence. I'm as subtle as elephants.
So I forget hesitance, stamp on religious reverence.
And disregard loveless experiments into the spiritual
That deny miracle and massage themselves whilst claiming to be
transcendently spiritual.
You would find more truth on the vitamin chart of a cereal
'Which would nourish and fortify your temple'
Or you could spend three hours breaking a sweat on a treadmill?
And still, have the abs that could achieve a cheap thrill.
And still, write pandering philosophy with an authentic ink quill
And kill, your heart and be led by your mind.
Become a slave to the times and live a life that never really tried …
To explore outside of the box.
Hiding behind academics' applause when the supernatural knocks.

MC McGladius, 'Shout your name', from the album 'Full Time'
www.29thchapter.org.uk

5

making Jesus famous

andy frost

I tend to walk around the park praying quite regularly. I find it is a really good place to be alone with God and listen to Him. My local park is a kind of 'suburban garden' that's packed with flowers, has nicely cut lawns and an occasional group of drunks. It is a pretty small park and when I pray I often walk around it several times. One spring afternoon, I was wandering around the park having a pray and asking God for more opportunities to share my faith. As I walked along the concrete pathway that circled round the park, I noticed a bunch of young men sat by some bushes drinking strong, cheap lager and smoking something that wasn't quite a normal cigarette. The characters looked pretty shady.

Whenever I passed these young men, my pace would tend to quicken as I feared some kind of confrontation and that would certainly not be good for my prayer life! I was on my second lap of the park, still praying for opportunities to talk about Jesus, when I began to approach them again. It was as I was approaching that I heard one of them shout sarcastically 'Nice sunglasses mate', obviously referring to my bright yellow sunnies that were perched on my head. I was feeling rather threatened by their sudden exclamation and hurt by the comment about my sunnies. My pace quickened again and my eyes were fixed to the floor. I was scared.

I was soon approaching them for my third time. I was now starting to pray that the park would suddenly grow so that I wouldn't have to receive any further insults whilst trying to be godly. This time one of them yelled out 'You won't get fit walking – you've gotta run to get fit!'. The comical line caused the other guys to laugh and it was at that moment that God spoke to me. He said 'Andy, stop praying for opportunities to share about me, and go and speak to them'. I immediately tried to correct God. This was not the plan. I wanted to speak to nice, middle class people not scary looking individuals drinking cheap lager early in the afternoon! As I was trying to reason my way out of speaking to these young men, I suddenly began to see God's perspective. He loved them for who they were and at that moment I was the one that he wanted to use to speak into their lives.

In response to their wisecrack about getting fit, I stopped in my tracks and turned to face them. Then from somewhere, I gave this classic opening line. 'I am not trying to get fit, I am talking to God and he told me to talk to you'. As I realized what I had just said, I felt like kicking myself but instead I walked over and sat down. The look of confusion on their faces told me just how strange my comment had seemed. Now *they* were scared and, within moments, I was being bombarded with questions about Jesus and I was sharing the gospel. The conversation flowed for half an hour and they agreed to come to church the following week. Although there was no dramatic conversion, this for me is what evangelism is all about!

Andy Frost

Epic tales

I love hearing those stories about 'old school' missionaries who preach in faraway countries that you only ever read about in geography lessons. You hear their tales of meeting tribes with pointy spears and warpaint, and about how they led entire civilizations to Christ. Then you hear those stories of evangelists in urban settings that get attacked and beaten up by gun-wielding gangsters. They, too, share stories of seeing entire gangs transformed as they enter into a relationship with God. Maybe these are the kind of images that you think of when you hear the word 'evangelist'. Or perhaps you conjure up a picture of a smartly-dressed preacher, in a shirt and tie, preaching on a big stage. A Billy Graham-type figure in a stadium stacked with people.

All of these examples of evangelists are great. But when I was growing up I often felt totally insignificant in comparison. I wanted exciting stories to share like they had but I often doubted if I could really be an evangelist. Who was I to share Jesus with people? Day by day, I would list excuses rather than giving it a go. I decided that when I knew the Bible well enough, when I could discern the voice of God fully and when I had undergone lots of training on mission, then I would be ready. But at present I just wasn't qualified.

> God poured his Spirit out to many desperate souls. Like thirsty men in the desert, they gleefully drank in the water of God's word. Even though I was just a teenager, the Lord enabled me to lead more than 2,000 to Jesus in my first year as a Christian.
>
> Brother Yun, *The Heavenly Man*
> (Monarch Publications, 2002)

Even the book of Acts scared me as I read mega-cool stories of Paul's mission trips that were stacked with adventure and tough times – Paul was shipwrecked, stoned by an angry mob and flogged for the gospel. Pretty full-on! But we need to remember that the word 'evangelist' simply means 'a messenger of good news'.

We must hold these stories in perspective – though we are all called to share Jesus this doesn't mean that we all have to move to Africa or book our local football stadium. God wants to use us, our relationships and our gifts to share our faith. Once we have entered a relationship with Jesus, we are called to 'go' and tell others.

'Go' But why don't we want to?

In Matthew, Mark, Luke and Acts, Jesus is recorded as giving the 'Great Commission' to the disciples. This commission is the instruction to go and tell others about Him. This is the last thing that Jesus is recorded as saying before He ascends into heaven, and this shows something of its importance. He did not tell us to build church buildings but to make disciples. This Great Commission is as relevant today as it was for the disciples 2,000 years ago. He has left the most amazing message in history in our hearts, and we, as the church, are called to go and share it.

> Therefore go and make disciples of all nations, baptising them in the name of the Father and of the Son and of the Holy Spirit, and teaching them to obey everything I have commanded you. And surely I am with you always, to the very end of the age.
>
> Matthew 28:19–20

The Great Commission is pretty clear on the whole issue of evangelism. We are told to 'go'. There is not much room for discussion here – Jesus doesn't ask, 'Do you fancy a bit of mission chaps?' He tells us to 'Go!' This indicates something of the importance and urgency of the task we have been given. But as with all aspects of discipleship, this is not some chore that we should feel obligated to do. Evangelism, being involved in God's plan to save the world, should be a joy and a privilege. It's pretty awesome that He allows us to be a part of this process.

So it is not merely because we are commanded to make disciples that we do evangelism or that we want to score brownie points with God. We have this life-transforming message in our hearts – what else are we going to do with it? We should *want* to go. We should *want* people to have meaning and purpose in their lives. We should *want* others to have their sins forgiven. We should *want* others to receive the gift of eternal life. This is such an important message we need other people to hear it. Jesus said 'No-one comes to the Father except through me' (Jn. 14:6).

The desire to share Jesus comes out of our relationship with Him. Our impetus for sharing the gospel should not be so that our church meetings look fuller or so that we can boast about how good we at evangelism. Our passion stems from knowing God. As we begin to know God better we begin to see others through His eyes – rather than seeing the outward, we start to see their hearts.

In the chapter on prayer (chapter 4), we looked at the process of listening to God. I believe that this is really important in knowing when there are evangelism opportunities that we need to take. We could go around stopping everyone that we pass in the street and trying to talk them into the kingdom – but this would be an exhausting exercise. Instead when our relationship is right with God we feel a certain nudge and end up in conversation. This is kingdom work. There are many sermons declaring the urgency and importance of mission, there are stacks of books on how to share your faith and when we look around our communities there are heaps of opportunities to talk about Jesus. Yet though many of us know that we should be sharing our faith, we don't. Day by day, as we choose not to share our faith, we become engulfed in guilt. Rather than focusing on why we should do evangelism, there are certain barriers that stop us from sharing – here are some of the questions that I have had to deal with in my personal faith sharing experience.

What is the gospel?

When I used to work in a department store, I would usually get stationed in menswear. I knew the products and understood how the whole measuring waistlines thing worked. I remember one week that they were short of staff and I got placed in the china department. What a mistake! I knew nothing about fine china and whenever I was asked questions, I would try and blag an answer or just shrug my shoulders.

How can we share the good news of Jesus if we don't fully understand the message? We need to know what the gospel is and what it means. More than that we need to know how to present it without all the jargon! I find the easiest way is with three words that I was always taught as a kid – thank you, sorry and please. Here's what I mean ...

> Strangely enough, the lens of grace reveals those outside the church in the very same light. Like me, like everyone inside the church, they too are sinners loved by God. Lost children, some have strayed very far from home, but even so the Father stands ready to welcome them back with joy and celebration.
>
> Philip Yancey, *What's So Amazing About Grace?*
> (Zondervan Publishing House, 2002)

Thank you – We need to thank God for creating us. He wants a relationship with us but we have all done things wrong (sin) and are imperfect. This stops us from entering a relationship with the perfect God. A sacrifice had to be made and Jesus, God's Son, came to earth to live a perfect life, to die on a cross and to rise again. We need to thank God for creating us and for sending His Son to die in our place (Jn. 3:16).

Sorry – We need to say sorry for the things that we have done that are wrong. This means changing our ways. We can never earn His forgiveness and it is only by God's grace that we enter into a relationship with Him (2 Cor. 5:20–21).

Please – We need to ask that God would forgive us, pour His Holy Spirit into our lives and give us His peace. As we do this we make Jesus Lord of our lives and start living for Him (Acts 2:38).

Romans 10:9 says that if we believe in our hearts and confess with our mouths, then we will be saved. We are saved from hell and have an eternal life with God. Our response of thanks for all that He has done is simply to live a life pleasing to God.

We can then give advice as to how this can be put into practice but we should never add on our own laws and make the gospel about earning God's love. It's so easy to give people a list of rules on how to behave. Though we can give advice, more than anything, we need to encourage new Christians to develop a relationship with God.

Once you know this basic message, you can be an evangelist – sharing Jesus. It is the key tool. You can move on to learn how to use spiritual gifts (e.g. healing, prophetic words, etc.) and how to use apologetics (giving a theological defence of Holy Scripture), but understanding the basic gospel message is the starting point.

> Evangelism is one beggar telling another beggar where to find bread.
>
> **Billy Graham (www.billygraham.org)**

The way in which we communicate this message has changed over the course of history but the message remains the same. People have adopted creative means to convey the message of the cross in a post-Christian culture. There is a wide spectrum of people using innovative ways to share Christ today. 'Eternal Riders' are a Christian extreme-sports clothing company that use their clothing label as a platform to talk about Jesus. 'Tough Talk' are a group of ex-bouncers and debt collectors that do power lifting to share their testimony. '29th Chapter' are a hip hop band that use rap to preach about Christ. All of these groups no longer sit in church waiting for people to come to them – instead they take the gospel to the world. Our church meetings should be a place of excitement as we share what God is doing in our lives and in our community – a place where we disciple new Christians. It should not be a place where we wait for the world to come to us.

As we go out into the world, it is important that we understand the context in which we are operating. This means that we need to know what is happening. We need to read magazines, watch TV and chat to people so that we can discern how we can share the gospel with them. Remember though, that all of these things need to be carefully balanced by our godly intake. I find the image of the preacher as someone with the Bible in one hand and a newspaper in the other is a helpful picture of the evangelist, too.

Recently, we have seen a surge in spirituality and I have found that people are more open to prayer than ever before. They want a spiritual experience and we as the church can offer them a relationship with God. I also find movies a great tool to open up conversations with others – conversations that go beyond the mundane. We need to be in the world but not of it (Jn. 17) – understanding it without compromising who we are called to be.

Be creative in the ways that you share Jesus, but don't allow the process to take priority over the message. Understandably, we want to share the gospel in a cringe-free style but we have to remember that no matter how we present the gospel, it will seem foolish in the world's eyes (1 Cor. 1:21–29).

What will people say when they find out I'm a Jesus freak?

I would reckon that the biggest issue that stops us from sharing Jesus is fear. Too often we live in fear of other people and what they think. We are so desperate to look cool and be accepted that we back down from sharing. We compromise our behaviour to be accepted. For example, sometimes we gossip about others in order to maintain our status in a group. As a church, too often we live in fear of the world – fear of what others will think of us.

A few years ago they introduced these big open-air toilets in central London. They were big plastic urinals and could be found on lots of street corners. If you wanted to use one, then everyone could watch. During the day time they were never used – people were too embarrassed. Yet when it came to evening time and as the pubs closed, there would be stacks of guys peeing into these plastic boxes. They had no shame and it was because they were drunk. When you are drunk, you lose your inhibitions and end up doing things that you would not normally do when sober.

It is interesting that as the disciples received the Holy Spirit at Pentecost, they were thought to be drunk. In fact the bars hadn't opened and they were not drunk on wine but on the Holy Spirit. God had empowered them to speak of Him and they had become bold! We need to allow God's Spirit to make us bold. I find the best way of doing this is to think in the cold light of day about what really matters, and to look at some of the situations when I am likely to back down and miss the challenge. I then pray through these up-and-coming circumstances and choose to stick to my guns, standing up for Jesus, when I encounter them.

We need to stop being so safe and make bold moves for Jesus! Too often we live in exclusive Christian cliques with churchy conversation. We talk about the latest Christian worship music and reminisce about the last Christian conference that we attended. We can become so inward-focused that we forget about the opportunities to share Christ in our communities.

'If sinners be damned, at least let them leap to Hell over our bodies. If they perish, let them perish with our arms about their knees. Let no one go there unwarned and unprayed for'

Charles Spurgeon (www.saltforsermons.org.uk)

Jesus was inclusive and crossed boundaries to chat to others. He spoke to prostitutes, tax collectors and ordinary people. We, as Christians, need to venture out into the big world and go beyond smiling at neighbours and shopkeepers. We need to get past the nice weather conversation.

Recently, I have decided that I want to live this unpredictable life. I want to talk to strangers. I want to pray for people at bus stops. I want to 'scare myself once a week' – not by looking in the mirror on a Monday morning or jumping off a block of flats but by pushing myself to interact with those around me.

Over the past month, my new 'scare myself' regime has led me into conversations with gothic hairdressers, an ex-drug-dealing debt collector, and flash businessmen. Sometimes the conversations open up into faith, life and death and other times I have ended up, for example, deep in conversation about the NHS ...! Whatever we talk about, I try to be Jesus to them.

> What will people think when they hear that I'm a Jesus Freak?
> What will people do when they find that it's true?
> I don't really care if they label me a Jesus Freak.
> There ain't no disguising the truth.
>
> D.C. Talk 'Chordant',
> from the album Jesus Freak, 1995

The amazing thing is that people are often very interested in what I have to share. Many have never knowingly met a Christian before and find it fascinating to hear my take on life. But there are also others that have mocked me. There are friendships that have not worked as people cannot accept what I believe and who I am striving to become. However, when the final curtain falls I want to be known as someone who knew God and made Him known.

Does The Gospel Actually Work?

The greatest joy, having been praying for and sharing with people, is seeing them become Christians. However, too many church communities do not see new people coming to Christ. Sometimes we go so long without seeing a new disciple that we forget that it still happens today. 'Well, maybe it happens in China, but not in our remote corner of the UK. People have money, family and Sky TV – the gospel just doesn't work.'

I was sat in the office one summer, preparing for a mission, doing the last little bits and pieces, when the phone went. I don't know if you have ever had an out-of-the-blue-type of phone call? I expected another mission-related query when the man on the other end of the phone explained that he was from Top of the Pops and that he wanted to film a famous band doing a gig in the church premises.

As he explained the concept over the phone, other people in the office could tell that I was getting excited. The guy on the phone then asked me to keep the whole thing under wraps, as he confirmed the details. I told him that I would do my best but have you ever tried to keep something so exciting under wraps? The excitement of finalizing food and transport details had been eclipsed with the prospect of Top of the Pops coming over. The phone went down and I jumped to my feet and shouted to everyone else in the office 'Guess what?' Then with a flurry of words, I described the phone call in detail. For the rest of the day, whenever I met or phoned anybody, I couldn't keep my mouth shut about what was happening.

It was during that mission that I realized how excited I had become about Top of the Pops and how unexcited I had become with the gospel. It is so easy to forget just how good the good news is!

Sometimes we become so casual with the gospel that we forget something of its greatness. We go into situations expecting no response because we ourselves have forgotten how powerful the message really is. When I meet a new Christian they are always so passionate and excited because they have this new revelation of the good news. When they share the message they expect things to happen.

We need to recapture this expectancy as we live our daily lives. As we spend time getting to know God better, He will start to build our expectancy. I love the Old Testament passage in 2 Kings 3. It always excites me. God's people end up stranded in the desert without enough water to march on to battle. They are in a dilemma and contemplate returning home. They enquire of the Lord through the prophet Elisha, who tells them to dig ditches in the desert. They are promised that if they dig ditches, although they will see no rain, the ditches will be filled with water the next day. Can you imagine digging ditches in the heat of a desert when there was no sign of rain – no clouds in the sky? Can you imagine digging in the belief that miraculously water would appear there the next day? Yet the people did what Elisha told them and began digging. Lo and behold, the ditches are full of water the following day.

They dug those ditches in faith that God would keep His promises. In the same way, we need to share the gospel with the expectancy that God will do the miraculous – that people will commit their lives to Jesus.

I have seen the gospel work in so many situations over the years I have been a Christian. I have seen young gang kids in the States come to Christ. I have seen my brother, Chris, who rebelled and got involved in fighting, drugs and sleeping around, come back to know Jesus. I have seen young people from Christian families come into their own relationships with God. I have seen an old woman in her eighties come to Christ. I have seen that the gospel works. These instances have helped me to remember to keep expecting God to move in every situation.

But how?

So you are up for sharing Jesus with people? But then comes the question – how on earth do we actually do it? The 'evangelism' word seems so scary! It is in fact not as hard as we often think and we are often doing it in many ways already. Every day there are opportunities to share Jesus. We just need to start looking for them. I find one of the easiest ways to understand evangelism is in the concept of sowing and reaping.

We live in a society where we want everything fast. Rather than working hard to earn money, people buy a lottery ticket – thinking 'it could be me'. Rather than chefing up a classic pasta dish, we head down to McDonalds. Rather than dieting and exercising to lose weight, why not get liposuction (nice!). I even get those emails that tell me – 'Why study hard when you can buy a degree on-line?.' Bargain.

I believe that in our culture, where we want immediate results and are often unwilling to put in the hard graft, if things don't happen quickly, we often can't be bothered at all. Some Christians have adopted this attitude when it comes to their faith. They want fast converts and if there is not an immediate response they give up or move on.

As I read the Bible, I am amazed how much it talks about sowing for a harvest. Though God sometimes does the miraculous, perhaps we as Christians don't always want to sow. I believe our problem is that we just don't get the whole sowing concept. The nearest most of us come to farming today is growing cress on cotton wool in primary school. Yet in Bible times, they had to work the land, turn the soil and endure the seasons. They were dependent on good crops and couldn't just pop down to ASDA for a pre-packaged salad or microwave lasagne.

The Bible calls us to sow in abundance: 'Whoever sows sparingly will also reap sparingly, and whoever sows generously will also reap generously' (2 Cor. 9:6). I want to see a bountiful harvest and I believe that we need to abundantly sow Jesus into our schools, our colleges, our workplaces and our homes. We need to sow love and truth where the world has sown hate and lies.

Pornography has devalued sex, media coverage of events has increased our fear, and magazines dictate our self-esteem and image. What has been sown is now being reaped. Yet we can see the tides change. We can see a different harvest. All we need to do is start sowing love. Though we may feel that we have so little to give, we can all sow love. We do not have to be great communicators or greatly experienced mission experts. Jesus spoke about the faith of a mustard seed being enough to move mountains. With the love that we can share, we can change lives. We can all sow the love that calls us to go the extra mile, the love that calls us to care for the marginalized and the poor, the love that is more than lip-service, the love that knows no limits.

Get out your pitch fork

Mission is about sowing. As I have no farming knowledge, I checked out a few agricultural websites to discover that there were two parts to sowing. First of all, there is the process known as preparing the soil. I have discovered that farmers turn the soil to allow the air to get in and that they use compost to enrich nutrient levels.

As Christians, we need to start preparing the soil which means preparing people's hearts. This involves challenging some people's misconceptions about Jesus and developing friendships of trust. For example, it saddens me when people sum up Christians as boring. Jesus was not boring and I want to be known as a person who is exciting to be around and who enjoys life. It also saddens me when Christians are thought of as hypocrites – people who say one thing yet do another. I want to be seen as a Christian who walks out what I speak. I want to be known as a person of integrity. It especially saddens me when Christians are thought of as religious – somehow pious and separate from the world. I want to show that Christians are not stuck in holy huddles but that we are people willing to get our hands dirty, willing to care for those who are hurting and marginalized.

> Preach the Gospel at all times. If necessary use words.
>
> **Accredited to St Francis of Assisi**
> **(www.quoteworld.org)**

We prepare the soil of people's hearts by showing people our lives. This is often known as *presence* evangelism. As people watch our lives, they should see that we live a very different lifestyle to those around us. I once heard a girl say 'If you watch my life, you will know that I am sold out for Jesus'. What a challenge that is. Though we are called to live lives that are different and thus provoke questions in people's minds, how often is this reality? As Christians we can too often become just like everyone else, with no mark of holiness on our lives as we get entangled in the world. In the book of Acts people saw the church as it is supposed to be, sharing all they had and looking after the poor (Acts 2:45).

Recently, I have been challenged by God about the amount of time I make myself available. We live in such a busy world and sometimes it appears that no-one has time for anyone else. We need to make time in our lives for godly interruptions. In the story of the Good Samaritan (Lk. 10:31–37), would we have made time for the man who was beaten or would we have been like the priest and the Levite – both too busy to care?

One summer I worked as a tour guide showing exchange students around London. There were no other Christians on the team. I didn't tell everyone that I was a Christian straight off but waited for it to come up in conversation. Then one day, whilst at Speakers' Corner, I sided with the Christian who was sharing the gospel. The other team leaders had had no idea that I was a Christian, but over the course of the next two days things began to make sense for them. They could now understand why I hadn't got drunk and why I didn't swear. Without realizing it, they had noticed the difference in the way that I lived my life.

Planting the seeds

The second part of the sowing process is planting seeds. We need to introduce the gospel message as words as well as deeds and not back down from the opportunities that we are given. This process is known as *proclamation* evangelism – proclaiming or speaking of Jesus. It may start with speaking certain aspects of truth into people's lives.

In the story of the woman at the well (Jn. 4) we see that Jesus prepares the woman's heart by going out of His way and being vulnerable by asking her for help. He speaks to her and cares for her. The fact that she was at the well at the heat of the day shows something of her place in that society – she was probably not liked! More than this, she was a Samaritan. Many religious people would have bypassed Samaria but Jesus went right through the region. Jesus then uncovered His identity. He sowed truth into her life, starting with the issue of her thirst.

> Jesus was born in a borrowed manger. He preached from a borrowed boat. He entered Jerusalem on a borrowed donkey. He ate the Last Supper in a borrowed room. And he was buried in a borrowed tomb. Now he asks to borrow the lives of Christians to reach the rest of the world. If we do not speak then he is dumb and silent.
>
> J. John, UK Focus, August 1997
> (Holy Trinity Brompton Church)

The problem is that when people start to uncover that we are Christians, we can often sometimes pass up the opportunities presented to us. I had a friend at university who had a long-term girlfriend. One night, one of the other guys quizzed him about his sex life. He told them that he was waiting till he was married before having sex. The other guys couldn't really understand why but my mate went no further. He backed down and missed the opportunity to share that his faith in Jesus was the reason why he was waiting till he was married.

We need to learn from Jesus and start planting snippets of testimony and the Bible that we can drop into people's lives. It is not necessarily right to wade in with the full gospel but to listen to their situations and then deposit truth. Testimony is a powerful tool for this. We need to practise sharing our story and how we have come to know Jesus. It is important that our story includes something of before we were a Christian, the process by which we became a Christian and what life has been like since. It might be that there was no specific landmark in your life when it all clicked into place, in which case, share about your journey with God and how you have come to know more of Him.

Testimony is never boring, as it is an example of how God has moved (Rev. 12:11). It helps people understand Jesus in a more personal way. Initially, we need to keep testimony short and we need to keep it clear from jargon and churchy language. We also need to keep it real. We do not need to glamorize our story or tell everyone that life has been one big ball since becoming a Christian. Testimony is a powerful tool and a great way to start sowing truth.

As you start sharing your faith, you will be bombarded with questions ranging from the validity of the Bible, other faiths and even the existence of aliens. We must never be afraid to admit that we are not sure. In our relationship with God there will always be things that we cannot fully comprehend. It is important that as the questions arise, we go and do our homework. Rather than letting these questions overwhelm us, we need to start studying to find some of the answers. Don't be afraid to receive questions and be spurred on by conversations.

Reaping what's been sown

So the sowing is about preparing the soil and planting the seeds. Therefore reaping is about harvesting the crop that has been produced from the seeds. In terms of this analogy, reaping is when people have heard the gospel and are willing to make a response.

One summer, I went shopping and rammed the car boot full of grub for the coming week. I then got into the car and started making my way home down a dual carriageway. As I was driving I began to feel a cool breeze – it was really refreshing but I couldn't quite understand where it was coming from. As I continued to speed up the dual carriageway, I looked in the mirror to see that the boot had swung open and that my shopping was, piece by piece, falling out of the car – the lettuce, then the potato, then the cartons of milk ...

Now I hate being embarrassed. And in my head I began to think that maybe I should keep driving – maybe no-one would notice. But the boot continued to empty as food disappeared into the road, and I realized that I had better stop! I pulled in and jumped out of the car to the sound of passing vehicles hooting! The road was littered with groceries. Cars were slowing down and people were wetting themselves with laughter.

I then began the rescue operation, jumping in between moving vehicles risking life and limb for the frozen peas and then the mayonnaise. It was such an embarrassing moment!

Everyone seems to hate being embarrassed and we go to extraordinary lengths to avoid looking silly. I think this embarrassment is sometimes what stops us from reaping. Sowing can be done without too much cringe factor but reaping really takes a step of faith, especially when it involves friends and family!

Sometimes I think we prefer sowing and are afraid to reap – when was the last time that you challenged someone to make a response? If we are going to start sharing the gospel, then we need to offer people the chance to respond.

There have been times when I have felt that it is right to give people an opportunity to respond to the gospel. And sometimes people chose to become Christians.

I meet some people who have had so much of Jesus sown into their lives and are now desperate to respond. In John 4:38 Jesus says to the disciples 'I sent you to reap what you have not worked for. Others have done the hard work, and you have reaped the benefits of their labour.' There is a harvest out there and we are working in partnership across the generations. 'One sows and another reaps.' As we sow we might not always see the fruits of our labour but there will be times when we will reap the fruit of someone else's work. The great truth is that God is in charge.

Holy ghost power – the vital component

The whole process of evangelism is teamwork. God uses us in His plans but He is in control. The mission field can seem so vast sometimes and we can feel guilty as we see all the people around us that are missing out on the opportunity to know God and have eternal life. What can we do about it?

We need to remember that only God can convert people, that only His Spirit can show someone that the gospel is true. We are merely called to pray and to live a life in obedience to Him – sharing the good news.

The Holy Spirit is vital in our lives. It is by the Holy Spirit that our lives are cleaned and sorted out. If we want to show Jesus in our presence evangelism, then we need to allow the Spirit to work in our lives so that people can see the fruit (Gal. 5:22–23). We need to receive the Spirit to give us the boldness to proclaim what God has done. We also need the Spirit to do the miraculous through us. This is what is known as *power* evangelism.

In 1 Corinthians 12, Paul writes about the gifts of the Spirit and about signs and wonders. All the way through the Gospels and book of Acts we see amazing things happening – people are healed, the dead come back to life and prophetic words lead people to Jesus. We need to allow God to use us to do the miraculous and this, too, stems from our relationship with Him.

> The filling with the Holy Spirit has two aspects in the book of Acts. One is a quality of life that should characterise all Christians. The other is an anointing for special challenges.
>
> Ajith Fernando, *Jesus Driven Ministry*
> (Crossway Books, 2003)

When I was 22, I established a mission in Cornwall called 'Dawn Patrol'. It was a mission to surfers primarily but also to clubbers, skaters and the wider party scene. As we were doing prep. for the mission, it dawned on me that we as church had often been so busy 'doing' mission with creative and good ideas that we had in fact failed to listen to God!

Therefore, on Dawn Patrol, though we put together a great programme of events, we were not tied to it. Each day of the mission we would pray and listen to hear the Father's perspective. Sometimes we scrapped entire parts of the programme to do what God wanted to do. It was not only the leadership group that spent time listening to God but every delegate was encouraged to spend time listening. As God spoke to individuals, the words were tested by the group and we saw great things happen.

It all stemmed from our relationship with God. For example, one team had two people who both separately felt quite sure that God was calling someone from the team to wait outside Woolworths. In faith, they sent one of the team to stand there. He waited for an hour and then someone came up to Him and said 'Excuse me, you have been stood here for a long time – what are you waiting for?'

The team member explained the situation to the stranger and God opened up a door. The team member had an amazing conversation and explained the gospel. He even got to pray for the stranger outside Woolies!

A few team members from another team were working on the beach and felt that God was calling them to go and pray for healing for an Asian family. They wandered over to them, they were unsure what exactly needed prayer. As they chatted to the young people, one of them explained that he was in agony as he had been stung twice in the foot by a weaver fish. They offered to pray for healing and immediately the young guy was jumping up and down, pain free. They then prayed for his brother who had his arm in a sling and who could not move his fingers. Again, the brother felt the pain had gone and began moving his fingers. As a result the whole family including the mother came to Christ!

> There is not a better evangelist in the world than the Holy Spirit.
>
> D.L. Moody (www.saltforsermons.org.uk)

But these amazing stories should not be limited to missions. They should be a part of our everyday life. Too often in our haste to 'do', we fail to wait for the inspiration of the Spirit. A key aspect of Acts was that the disciples waited upon God before doing. They did not try and preach in the streets about all that had happened until the Spirit came at Pentecost. I believe that God wants to do more miraculous things in our generation – it is just a case of waiting upon Him. Let's spend more time practising in the church and then taking it out onto the streets. The Holy Spirit is therefore the vital component for mission.

Timing ...

I had prayed for my schoolmate at least five times. I then invited him into my house for a Coke. Now he had no immediate escape and sitting on the couch next to me, I launched into my rehearsed three point gospel sermon. I meticulously explained all about Jesus and then sat patiently for the response. I expected him to get on his knees and shout, 'Alleluia! I believe!'. His response was somewhat different to what I had expected. His eyes glazed over and he asked me what my favourite ice cream flavour was!

'Err ... excuse me,' I thought to myself, 'you can't talk about ice cream, I have just explained salvation'. I couldn't understand it, I had done everything right – text book stuff. Why hadn't my mate become a Christian there and then?

Salvation is all about God. There are instances in the Bible when we see people respond to Jesus immediately. God is not trapped by formulas and sometimes we can see immediate results. The woman at the well is a great example of this. She is so excited when Jesus reveals to her who He is that she runs to the town to tell everyone else, leaving her water behind. Her response was immediate.

On the other hand, there are instances when salvation takes time. My school mate has yet to choose Jesus and though I keep sowing into his life I have not seen him come to faith. Yet we can take hope from men such as Nicodemus. He was a man who got so much right. He had the right desire. He came to the right person, Jesus. He asked the right question, 'How can I be born again?'. Yet when Jesus explained what Nicodemus had to do, he made no immediate response (Jn. 3). However, later in the gospels we read that Nicodemus stands up for Jesus when he challenges the Sanhedrin with the question, 'Does our law condemn a man without first hearing him to find out what he is doing?' (Jn. 7:40–51). And later, after Jesus' death, we read that Joseph was accompanied by Nicodemus, the man who earlier had visited Jesus at night. Nicodemus brought a mixture of myrrh and aloes for Jesus' body. The seed had been sown but the crop took time to be cultivated.

The church is all about partnership. Seeds are planted and harvests are reaped across generations, across denominations and across cultures. We trust that God is sovereign and that one day we will rejoice together.

Disciples not just converts

Our job does not end with leading someone in a short prayer of commitment to Jesus. The Great Commission calls us to make disciples. This means nurturing new believers in their faith, helping them to know God.

RECAP

Faith-sharing is about allowing God to use all that we are

Faith-sharing is about knowing Jesus

Faith-sharing is about boldness

Faith-sharing is about expecting

Faith-sharing is about sowing

Faith-sharing is about reaping

Faith-sharing is about the Holy Spirit

Faith-sharing is about making disciples

Practical tips

- Random acts of sacrificial kindness can work wonders e.g. wash a neighbour's car, bake the local policeman a cake!?

- Read your Bible in public! People will often give you weird looks and sometimes they will be so intrigued that they will ask you questions.

- When people tell you that they are having a difficult time or that someone is sick, offer to pray for them.

- Write a questionnaire for your local church that looks at people's views on faith and Jesus. Then go out onto the streets and get some filled in. As you are talking to people, use the questions to get into deeper conversations. The results from the survey will enable your local church to structure mission initiatives more effectively.

- Buy or create Christian clothing that will provoke questions (www.eternalriders.com, www.christian bandits.co.uk).

- Scare yourself by trying to start a conversation with a complete stranger!

- Write your own personal tracts with testimony and photo. Then laminate them to give a more professional look.

- Make a hit list of three people that you want to know Jesus. Pray for them daily and try and create opportunities to share Jesus with them.

- Text someone with a verse that you think is appropriate for them.

- Go on a short-term mission. Check out the opportunities that are available in the UK and worldwide varying from one week to a few months. (To start your search, have a look at www.sharejesusinternational.com, www.ywam.org and www.christianvocations.org).

- Make a list of the reasons why you don't share your faith and then talk and pray them through with a friend.

- Practise sharing your testimony with a friend or in the mirror. There is also the matchstick challenge: light a match and begin sharing your story – you must finish before the match goes out (or burns your fingers).

- Spend time reflecting on 2 Corinthians 5:16–21 and Mark 4:1–20.

- Spend time listening to God every day and ask Him for words of knowledge as you are talking to people and then have the boldness to share them!

- Write the words SOW and REAP on your diary to remind you to be faith-sharing.

Further reading

To get started ...

Becoming a Contagious Christian, Hybels, Strobel, Mittelberg, Zondervan Publishing House, 2002

Calling Out, J. John, Authentic Lifestyle, 2000

Challenging Lifestyle: Study Guide, N. Gumbel, HTB Alpha Resources

The Art of Connecting, Roy Crowne and Bill Muir, Authentic Lifestyle, 2003

Out of the Comfort Zone, George Verwer, Authentic Lifestyle, 2000

What's So Amazing About Grace?, Philip Yancey, Zondervan Publishing House, 2002

Xcelerate: The Evangelist's Heartbeat, Andy Hawthorne and Matt Wilson, Scripture Union Publishing, 2002

In depth ...

Evangelism Made Slightly Less Difficult, Nick Pollard, InterVarsity Press, 1998

Mere Christianity, C.S. Lewis, Zondervan Publishing House, 2001

Out of the Saltshaker & Into the World: Evangelism as a Way of Life, Rebecca Manley Pippert, InterVarsity Press, 1999

Power Evangelism, John Wimber and Kevin Springer, Hodder & Stoughton Religious, 1997

Reaching Generation Next: Effective Evangelism in Today's Culture, Lewis A. Drummond, Baker Books, 2002

Sharing Jesus in the New Millennium, Rob Frost, Scripture Union Publishing, 2000

Sowing, Reaping, Keeping: People-Sensitive Evangelism, L. Singlehurst, Crossway Books, 1995

I'm tired I'm frustrated I'm not capable I'm not motivated I'm terrified I'm not ready I'm not encouraged I'm selfish I'm lazy I don't want to fail.

He's strong He's comforting He's capable He's motivating He's powerful He's ready He is encouragement He's ready He's selfless He's pursuing He will never fail.

I don't know I don't care I can't touch people I'm not strong I'm not loving I'm guilty I'm ashamed.

He knows all He cares about all He can touch lives He's mighty He loves abundantly He's pure and He's perfect.

I am human.
He is God. And His strength is made perfect in my weakness.

I am therefore completely dependent and that's exactly how He wants it.

MARCY BURNHAM

6

bringing in the kingdom

jo wells

Thousands of miles from England, I walked down the dusty dirt track in a shantytown in Lima, Peru.

Every morning drunks would line the streets. Half-built shacks and crumbling shops stretched as far as the eye could see. Each day ten white students would walk down the road with the staring eyes of the locals fixed upon us. 'Hola Gringo!' would greet us every morning as puzzled faces looked on to see the strangest spectacle they had ever known. Why would ten rich white people work in the dusty, dirty suburbs of Lima, for no money and no thanks? They couldn't understand it.

Building a community centre in the heart of the shantytown was hard work. We had no building skills, no construction knowledge, we didn't even speak Spanish. But we wanted to communicate God's love to these people in a way they could understand. Next door there were a couple of kids that would watch us wide-eyed through the fence. One of our team started playing with them one day – pulling silly faces and playing catch. The next day we had six kids hanging around, wanting the gringos to pay them some attention. By the end of week we were overrun. Kids were everywhere. What had started out as a simple building project had turned into the most successful kids club ever!

We soon learnt simple Spanish words like 'Vuelta! Vuelta!' meaning 'Spin us round like an aeroplane!'. This was their favourite game. They learnt simple English like 'sit down, sit down!' which was our favourite game! Each day we hugged, played, sat and sang with the kids of the shantytown. They smelt. They had dirty nit-infested hair. They wore the same filthy rags every day of the week, but we didn't care. We soon learnt that no-one, not even their own families, showed love to them as we were doing – and they certainly never expected the gringos to do so.

On our last day one of the parents invited the team to their house for lunch. As we crowded into the half-built lounge, the mother explained the community's feelings towards our work through a cascade of tears. They thought at first that we had come to steal their children. It was the only way they could make sense of what we were doing – white Europeans coming into their homes and taking their children from them. But as the weeks went on, they came to see that they were wrong, we had no such agenda. In broken English, this mother thanked us. 'Thank you for teaching us how to love our children.'

Jo Wells

I have never been so humbled in my life. How could I or any of my team have taught this mother how to love her children? But as I sat there in that small dank and dark front room, I came to understand that it wasn't anything that we had done. Jesus' love for those children had shone out of us. A love that said 'No matter who you are or what your situation is, Jesus loves you just as you are.' Jesus breaks down every social barrier, every political situation. His love transcends it all. And through His love our status in life is transformed. During His time on earth He demonstrated God's heart for the marginalized. He shunned the rich and the privileged, and favoured those for whom society had no time. Justice and love were at the heart of Jesus' mission on earth. He showed us how to love and when He returned to the Father He gave us the responsibility to continue His work.

Paint a picture of justice

'Religion that God our Father accepts as pure and faultless is this: to look after orphans and widows in their distress and to keep oneself from being polluted by the world' (Jas. 1:27). We live in a world where the gap between the richest people and the poorest is huge and getting bigger literally every minute. Laws, aspects of trading, business, or commerce in general has been fixed for centuries so the rich can get richer … and stuff anyone else out there. It's a dog-eat-dog world, and if you're not prepared to walk over a few hundred starving families to get a cheap cup of coffee, then you are one of remarkably few.

Throughout the Bible, one thing is abundantly clear: God's passion has always been for justice. If you tore out all the passages in the Bible that discuss God's heart for justice, the Bible would literally fall apart. Time and time again God calls His people to care for those that the world won't care for. We are to be the instruments of God's heart, to love the world enough to die for it.

How often have we heard in church that God's way and the world's way are utter opposites? God's heart for justice is the clearest demonstration of this. The gospel we carry is all about God's kingdom being established. Catch a glimpse of that kingdom and you will see how far we have fallen from that ideal.

One of the most stunning pictures the Bible paints is that of Jerusalem, the perfect city. A city where God is King and everyone is welcome. Every time I read Revelation 22, I get excited again. One day He will bring His kingdom to earth and everything will be put right. All the things that are wrong in the world will be restored to how God wanted them to be. Jerusalem is the symbol of that kingdom. Jesus proclaimed that the kingdom of God is at hand. The kingdom of God is within each one of us that declares Jesus as Lord. The kingdom of God where all people can find sanctuary. Are we offering sanctuary to those that need it? Do we even know how to?

Jesus declared His mission on earth as the fulfilment of the prophecy found in Isaiah 61: 'The Spirit of the Lord is on me, because he has anointed me to preach good news to the poor. He has sent me to proclaim freedom for the prisoners and recovery of sight for the blind, to release the oppressed, to proclaim the year of the Lord's favour' (Lk. 4:18–19). Jesus' ministry spoke into every aspect of human life.

Good news to the poor

I have been to many churches that meet on council estates. I've walked past homes and listened to the cries of a mother screaming at her child to get out of her f-ing sight. I've seen graffiti covering every wall with obscene pictures and comments. The aftermath of a Saturday night gets strewn across the roads, broken bottles, takeaway packets, syringes all over the place. Destruction and disillusionment abound.

One church I visited meets right in the middle of such an estate. Large estate cars line the car park, and a security guard is hired to protect the congregation's property. I press the buzzer to announce my arrival, and am allowed to enter once I have been vetted. I walk into the sanctuary as the organ strikes up the first traditional hymn. The congregation is made up entirely of white, middle class, middle-aged and elderly people, most of whom travel a fair distance to worship here every Sunday.

Another church greets me with a cartoon poster of a stereotypical burglar in a black and white top and swag bag swung over his shoulder. Beneath his picture a caption reads: 'Beware! Non-members about!'

No-one from the estates surrounding these two churches attends the meetings. I don't stop to wonder why.

> The Church is the only institution that exists for those who are not yet its members.
>
> William Temple, Archbishop of Canterbury, 1942–44
> (Mark Littleton, *Tales of the Never Ending*,
> Moody Press, 1991)

Jesus declared that He was not here for the righteous but for sinners 'It is not the healthy that need a doctor, but the sick' (Mt. 9:12). Yet so often our churches are dedicated to making us feel safe and welcome but forgetting those on the outside who desperately need to hear the good news.

Often when discussing the Christian response to social justice our minds run straight to dusty mud huts in Africa, or to the war-torn Middle East. We forget that social justice is just as important, just as necessary, on our very own doorstep.

William Booth didn't forget this. As a Methodist minister his overwhelming desire was to see the lost saved and social reform in Britain. Caring for the homeless, the drunks and the poor at a time when there were no social services, no option of collecting the Giro, he resigned his position in the Methodist Church and worked ceaselessly to bring the kingdom of God about in this nation. He established the Salvation Army, which by the time he died, was active in fifty-eight countries. It spoke a language that Victorian England understood. No hypocrisy, just straight down the line gospel preaching accompanied by active faith lived out in the community. People flocked to the Salvation Army banner. They flocked to Jesus.

> While women weep as they do now, I'll fight. While little children go hungry as they do now, I'll fight. While men go to prison, in and out, in and out, as they do now, I'll fight. While there is a drunkard left, while there is a poor lost girl on the streets, while there remains one dark soul without the light of God, I'll fight – I'll fight to the very end.
>
> William Booth
> (www.stpetersnottingham.org/heroes/booth.htm)

We meet people every day who need to know the good news of Jesus. They need to hear it and they need to be faced with the reality of it in their lives. God cares about the whole person, their soul, their health, their hopes and their hurts. Jesus embodied that fact every day. Today we are being transformed into His likeness. Jesus is with us every day. We are part of the kingdom of God. We are called to bring good news to those that need it.

Proclaim freedom for the prisoners

Jesus came to set us free. Biblical freedom is freedom from sin and it promises the opportunity to live in the fullness of all that sin has held us back from. The spiritual freedom we hear discussed in churches is utterly paramount, but sin has trapped more than people's souls. Freedom is something that every person deserves.

- Freedom to life
- Freedom of speech
- Freedom from wrongful imprisonment
- Freedom from addiction

Around the world there are countless people held behind bars for their political or social views. Human rights are being denied in many countries. Injustice from governments is widespread and aided by apathy and ignorance. We as Christians have a responsibility to give a voice to those who are silenced. Too often we turn a deaf ear.

From my friendship groups, I have learnt how easy it is to be trapped in something. I love my friends, but sometimes it feels like we're a living agony aunt page! I have friends that have suffered from depression, self-harming, eating disorders, child abuse, sexual abuse, sexual confusion and drug abuse. Imprisonment does not necessarily mean being behind bars. Each one of these friends knows what it is to be in prison. Utterly trapped and utterly unable to set themselves free.

One girl was terrified of admitting to people the things she was doing in her life. She was sure that they would pass judgement on her and condemn her for her lifestyle. The situation she was in was perpetuated by her fear to ask for help. She knew the sex and the drugs were wrong, but she didn't know how to stop. I would spend hours on the phone with her, for a period of months.

Not once did I condone her actions, but neither did I say she was bad for doing it. Slowly, Jesus was speaking love and grace into her life. She was being affirmed for who she was and gradually she gained the strength to walk away from all that was holding her back. I used to get so frustrated sometimes that I couldn't just tell her the gospel straight and sort her out in two minutes flat. But she didn't need to hear a speech, she needed to experience love.

Do we come with an agenda that through our actions we can preach the gospel, or do we act simply because we care?

> Let your continual mercy, O Lord, enkindle in your Church the never-failing gift of love. That, following the example of your servant William Wilberforce, we may have grace to defend the children of the poor, and maintain the cause of those who have no helper. For the sake of Him who gave his life for us, your Son our Saviour Jesus Christ, who lives and reigns with you and the Holy Spirit, one God, now and for ever, Amen.
>
> *Lesser Feasts and Fasts* (Church Pub Inc, 2003)

Recovery of sight for the blind

Jesus spent 90 per cent of His recorded ministry on Earth healing people. As a response to those with faith, or on behalf of those who could not ask for themselves, Jesus continually demonstrated the reality of the kingdom of God as being far more than simply a 'heaven thing'. He showed us that the kingdom was about living a full life, a whole life, here on earth.

After Pentecost, the disciples, filled with the Holy Spirit, demonstrate an even greater ability to heal than the one Jesus had shown. Peter's shadow would even heal the sick. This is the fulfilment of the promise Jesus made: '... anyone who has faith in me will do what I have been doing. He will do even greater things than these ...' (Jn. 14:12).

The gift of healing is one of the spiritual gifts that Paul discusses in 1 Corinthians 12. As we discussed in chapter 4, the Holy Spirit is living and active and the gifts He offers are still available today. Praying for healing is a scary thing. What if nothing happens? What if someone gets their hopes up and God doesn't come through? We need to have faith in Jesus. Imagine if He does come through. Imagine seeing a blind woman see, a lame man walk! I remember a friend of mine jumping up and down, simply because his headache went. The kingdom of God is at hand, and healing marks its arrival. Let's risk it, let's step out in faith and see if Jesus meets us there.

As well as the miraculous, Jesus also works through the mundane. Caring for people may seem slightly less dramatic. But showing love to people is an amazingly effective way of opening their eyes to the love of Jesus. My mate got sick once and couldn't get out of bed. The rest of my house kinda forgot all about her and just got on with their daily lives. But I stayed. I phoned the doctor for her, got her prescriptions for her, made her food, and bought her magazines. It wasn't glamorous, she didn't fall on her knees crying, 'I repent! Jesus is real!' But she thanked me. She noticed that I had gone the extra mile.

Recovery of sight for the blind means opening people up to the reality of the kingdom of God. Whether it be literal healing, caring or praying that people will see the truth in Jesus, all are about the equality that Jesus demonstrated. The equal opportunity of all people to become whole in God.

Release the oppressed

The war in the Eastern region of Congo resumed two weeks ago. About 30,000 people, the majority kids and women, are refugees on Burundi territory now. Burundi which is just turning a corner after eleven years of civil war. Last year we were classified as the second poorest nation in the world. I want to say that these refugees are in a very critical situation. They have no food, no drinking water, no blankets, etc. Last week, I visited one of the centres where these people are gathered, I felt so sad and angry. Africa is dying just because of poor leadership. Congo is so rich a nation with all kinds of resources but people are dying every day with guns and hunger. I cried to see them fighting for water to drink. I decided not to go there again as I have nothing to give them but I am praying, trusting God for a miracle.

Simon Guillebaud, Extract from Newsletter 30
(www.greatlakesoutreach.org)

Jesus turned the world upside down by never doing or saying what was expected of Him. Israel was waiting for a Saviour. They had been under foreign rule for centuries, and under Roman occupation since 63 BC. They were an utterly oppressed nation clinging to the promise of God that He would send someone to set them free.

Jesus declared that He was the one that they had been waiting for. But He was not going to be some great warrior king. He was going to die for freedom, not fight for it.

Politically, Jesus was playing a dangerous game. As God's ambassador, He was sent to complete the Scriptures that declare Israel as God's chosen nation. But God's agenda has always been bigger than that. God wants the whole world to be in a relationship with Him. So to release the oppressed meant far more than doing so for the nation of Israel only.

Perhaps the easiest way to understand this is to look at one of the challenges the Pharisees made to Jesus that we read about in Matthew 22:15–22. They set a trap for Him, asking whether Jews should pay taxes to the Romans. They were asking whether Jesus would support the oppression of the Jewish people by financially supporting the oppressor. Surely God would say it was wrong? But it was a double trap because the Pharisees brought with them allies of the Romans so that if Jesus were to say that it was wrong, He would be arrested for treason. It was a no-win situation. Either He supported oppression or He risked imprisonment.

Jesus replied, 'Give to Caesar what is Caesar's, and to God what is God's' (Mt. 22:21). His answer was that justice and freedom would come through God, not futile arguments.

Isaiah 1:17 says, '... Seek justice, encourage the oppressed, defend the cause of the fatherless, plead the case of the widow.' God never supports social and economic oppression. His heart is always for freedom. But throughout the Bible, we are told to pray for our persecutors and to honour those in authority. In Romans, Paul tells us to submit to those in authority as God gives them their authority over us. However, we read in Acts how John and Peter refused to stop preaching about Jesus, even when it became illegal. Their argument was 'We must obey God rather than men!' (Acts 5:29).

So what should we do when on the one hand we are told to honour those in power whilst on the other we are told to obey God not man, and defend the rights of the oppressed?

There have been varying views about what it is to defend the rights of the oppressed. They range from the so-called permitted violence in liberation theology, to the apathetic 'tut-tut!' found in many evangelical churches.

Last year a family of Kosovan asylum seekers got deported illegally from our community. One minute they were round at our homes playing football with us. The next minute they were gone, no warning, just tears in the aftermath. Should we have just shrugged our shoulders and sighed 'What a shame'? Should we have stormed the Houses of Parliament with machine-guns and demand them back? No. Instead we did the only thing we could do – we pleaded their case.

We kicked up the biggest fuss we could. We marched in protest, we spoke to newspapers, radio and TV stations. We raised money for lawyers, we went to court. We did not stop until our case was heard. Our government had mistreated those it should have helped and we were going to fight until it was put right.

Politicians asked us to be quiet. But we would not be quiet. We were speaking on behalf of those who could not speak for themselves.

After eight months, the Home Office admitted their mistake one week before our court case was to be heard. Within six days the family were home.

Silence lies at the heart of oppression. The oppressed are unable to speak for themselves. Christians are charged with the responsibility to speak up for them. Prejudice and persecution is rife in our society. Poverty, alternative lifestyles, religious beliefs, nationality all lead to people suffering needlessly in life. Oppression is simply a fancy word for bullying. We need to stand up to the bullies, shower them with grace and pray for their conviction to change.

Proclaim the year of the Lord's favour

What if you were to wake up one morning and know that you didn't owe anybody anything? All your family's debts have been cleared. The house you live in is yours, not the bank's, not the landlord's. That morning you didn't owe anybody any favours, all the clothes in the cupboard were yours, all the CDs on your shelf and the DVDs on the floor. The slate was clean. How amazing would that be?

That is the morning that begins the 'year of Jubilee', the 'year of the Lord's favour'. Old Testament law declares that every fifty years there should be a year where everybody's debt is removed. Slaves set free, land returned to owners. Jesus declared that His coming was the year of the Lord's favour.

Some people suggest that Jesus was talking about the debt we owe God. That through Jesus' death, our sins are removed, the slate wiped clean and we are restored to an equal footing.

There is no denying the truth of this. But there is also a physical, actual call on Christians to proclaim the year of the Lord's favour. Jesus commands us to 'Give to everyone who asks you, and if anyone takes what belongs to you, do not demand it back' (Lk. 6:30). We need to develop an attitude of holding our possessions lightly. They come from God, and He can distribute them however He likes.

The most striking modern example of this must be the Jubilee 2000 and 'Drop the debt' campaigns. Lobbying governments from around the world to cancel third world debt, Jubilee 2000 managed to gain 24 million signatures and an agreed cancellation of $110bn of debt after only four years of campaigning. Today there are millions of people attending schools and receiving healthcare because of the year of the Lord's favour.

One of my lasting memories is of the Treasury official who complained to me about the number of letters he received from Jubilee 2000 supporters. 'They were well-informed,' he said, 'too damn well informed'. People wrote about poor countries' debt-to-export ratios; about their pre-cut-off-date debt; about whether it was correct to base predictions on the net present value as opposed to the nominal value of the debt. This official was particularly struck by a letter challenging the Treasury's assertion that Uganda had had massive debt relief from her last Paris Club re-scheduling – and pointing out that only Uganda's pre-cut-off-date debt had been included. 'The letter,' he said, 'was written on pink notepaper, with a little posy of roses in the corner! Who are these people?'

Ann Pettifor (www.jubilee2000uk.org)

When we start to care more about people than our possessions, things change. When we care about people we've never met, God changes things. Jubilee 2000 was a success because people were prepared to put the effort in to see things put right.

Take a look at your community. What is wrong with what you see? Does everyone have enough? Are homes cared for? Schools and hospitals sufficiently resourced? Is the council serving the whole community or a select few? We need to ask ourselves what we can do about it. How much effort are we prepared to put in to see things change?

The social gospel

About 100 years ago there was a big split in the church. On the one hand people were arguing that the call of a

Christian was to love their neighbour. They argued that people would come to know Christ through us 'embodying' the gospel. Other Christians argued that the gospel must be preached. Ensuring eternal salvation was the primary task of the church, all other actions were secondary. That has led to the big divide we are faced with today. Love in a social context versus preaching the word.

> In the Scriptures we are not advised to love our neighbour, we are commanded. The church needs to lead the way here, not drag its heels. The government needs guidance. We discuss; we debate; we put our hands in our pockets. We are generous even. But, I tell you God is not looking for Alms; God is looking for action. He is not just looking for our loose change – he's looking for a tighter contract between us and our neighbour.
>
> Bono, Anthony DeCurtis © 1996–2004 by (www.macphisto.net)

Biblically, however, the two were never meant to be separated. The gospel is about living as a community that personifies the kingdom of God and it's about the relationship available for us as individuals to be children of God. Peter commands us to live such good lives that people will enquire after our life choices (1 Pet. 2:12). Paul commands us to preach the word (2 Tim. 4:2), that we are to proclaim the name of Jesus at all times. Both camps were right – but somewhere along the line things got forgotten. Or maybe things just got too hard.

There can be an attitude that proclamation evangelism is the most important aspect of the Christian life. That God only really cares about people's spiritual situation.

And anyway, it's too hard to try and change their physical situation. Billions of dollars of debt. War rife around the world. Dirty politics on both sides, and Joe Bloggs gets stuck in the middle. You can kinda see why it's easier to talk about salvation in heaven rather than the kingdom of God being established on earth. But our God promises to move when we share His heart for justice. The task is huge, but if you look throughout history God has honoured that promise. Insignificant people who have faith in a completely powerful, totally sovereign God, have dared to believe they can move the mountain of injustice and send it crumbling into the sea. Dare we believe it too?

What's our responsibility?

I look around in the world, and I see Christians desperately wanting God to be God, to come and fix all the things that are wrong in our lives. Why hasn't He moved? Why does He not do all the things that He says He will and that I know He is capable of? One of the most frustrating things about God is that He has tied His own hands. He has granted us freedom, freedom to choose His way or our way. But every choice we make has a consequence.

Isaiah 58 details a rebuke from God. The religious people at the time were praying and fasting, doing all the 'good holy' stuff, but throughout the week they were oppressing people rather than helping them. They were crying out to God to honour them and fulfil His promises over them, but not living out what He had asked of them. God answers them, and says that the words they speak must be matched with their actions.

The consequence of our apathy is the limitation of God's activity in our lives and the lives of our neighbours. We limit our sight to our own lives and wonder why God seems so silent.

'This is the type of fasting I have asked for: getting the heavy-duty cutters on the chains of injustice. Chainsawing through the ropes holding down the oppressed. Isn't religion about spreading food out including the starving? Isn't it about putting a roof over the heads of the refugee? About putting clothes on the naked? About not turning a blind eye on your own family? You do this and you'll be like the sun after a long dark night.

Isaiah 58:6–9, *The Street Bible*

Statistically speaking, there are over 2 billion Christians in the world. A third of the world professes to be of the Christian faith. Now even if the actual number of people

Now, for all its failings and its perversions over the last 2,000 years – and as much as every exponent of this faith has attempted to dodge this idea – it is arguably the central tenet of Christianity: that everybody is equal in God's eyes. So you cannot, as a Christian, walk away from Africa. America will be judged by God if, in its plenty, it crosses the road from 23 million people suffering from HIV, the leprosy of the day. What's up on trial here is Christianity itself. You cannot walk away from this and call yourself a Christian and sit in power. Distance does not decide who is your brother and who is not. The church is going to have to become the conscience of the free market if it's to have any meaning in this world – and stop being its apologist.

Anthony DeCurtis © 1996–2004 222.macphisto.net

following Jesus is far less, that is still a fairly sizeable force for the advancement of God's kingdom. Imagine what would happen if every Christian took hold of God's heart for justice. Imagine if every Christian refused to buy unfairly-traded goods. Imagine if every Christian refused to support an unjust government. Imagine if every Christian cared for the people in their community, not just claimed they did on a Sunday.

One man totally changed the world. One! Jesus Christ. But there have been many other individuals throughout history who lived amazing lives. Martin Luther King, Isaac Newton, John Stuart Mill, Mother Teresa. All because they dared to think that they might be able to change things.

There are millions of 'ones' living in communities every day. Imagine how much you could change with God on your side.

I work in a school, helping out in their vulnerable students department. They have loads of those inspirational posters on the walls. You know the ones. Something profound gets written over a striking sunset or a deserted tropical beach. They are there to remind the students that 'It's OK to be smart' and 'Respect begins with you'. Normally I'm not the hugest fan of those posters but there's one that always makes me stop and think: 'Those who dare to dream – achieve. Those who aren't afraid to fail – succeed.' Too often it feels as if we are defeated before we even begin. We forget how big God is, and how He promises to move when we do. His kingdom is being established every day. But we are the agents advancing it. If our hands don't do anything then nothing will ever get done. Nothing will change.

If fear is the root cause of why we don't share our faith, then I believe apathy is the reason we don't get on and do something!

I was in Year 10 and Julie walked into the classroom holding the latest issue of *Amnesty International* magazine. Opening it up, I had never heard of some of the places or people it talked about, but I quickly realized that there were many people out there who were living a life that would probably kill me and I wasn't doing a lot about it.

Amnesty had a simple answer – one they said anyone could do – just write a letter. Tell the people in charge what you think of what they are doing. If enough people write they will take notice and things will change. Easy.

But I never quite got round to writing the letter. Worse still, when Amnesty were doing a campaign, *they* would write the letter. All I was expected to do was sign and post it. But I never quite made it to the post-box. The simplest way of acting on social justice and even I couldn't manage it.

> God will do nothing but in answer to prayer.
>
> John Wesley, *A Plain Account of Christian Perfection* (Broadman & Holman, 1999)

It all starts with prayer! As we said in chapter 4, prayer is the communication between God and us. It is the method by which God transfers His heart's concerns to us. If apathy is the reason we don't do anything we need to pray for God's heart to be restored in us.

I remember once praying the most dangerous prayer. I asked God to show me the world as He sees it, and break my heart, as His has been broken. That was a risky thing to do, and over the next week I was constantly being struck by a world that didn't know God. The absence of God was so obvious in the lives people were living. As I walked down streets I could only pray that God would put things right, that God would fix things. Instead of caring about where I was at, the focus of my prayers became other people. I would look people in the eye, instead of hoping that they wouldn't ask me for money. My priorities began to change. I began to hurt for people's situations, and me with nothing to offer began to see how I might be able to help.

Prayer is the way God stirs us to action. If we want things to change, we have got to pray more, because all change comes from God.

Where have you settled?

The call for justice is not about feeling guilty because you haven't done enough. However, the closer we get to God, the greater our understanding and our need to be like Him becomes. The question is can we call ourselves Christian, here in the world to do God's work, if we are not searching after His heart? The call of social justice cost Jesus His life. He was willing to die to see God's kingdom rightfully established. Is life too comfortable for us to reach out for those who need us? Have we settled where it's safe? Are we willing to die for the sake of justice? Are we even prepared to put ourselves out a bit? Embarrassment, fear or apathy render us unwilling to act. If it doesn't affect us personally it just doesn't seem worth the effort.

Let's get out of the bubble and go into the world. We are called to embody the kingdom of God. As the African proverb says; 'If you think you're too small to make a difference you've never been in bed with a mosquito.'

RECAP

Justice is in God' heart

Justice is what Jesus demonstrated

Justice is our commission

Justice needs to be shown throughout our lives

Justice is about equality

Justice is about freedom

Justice is about wholeness

Justice is about responsibility

Practical applications

- Check out campaign websites to see how you can join up with a massive body of people.

- Buy a copy of the *Big Issue*.

- Chat to the person on the street. If you don't feel comfortable giving beggars money, why don't you buy them a cup of tea, or just sit down on the ground and have a chat?

- Check out the fair trade ethos of your church, coffee shop and supermarket and encourage them to sell fairly-traded goods.

- Adopt a granny – go to the local old people's home and play a game of cards with someone. Ask your pastor if there are any shut-ins in your area that would appreciate being visited.

- Adopt a child – like a granny, see if there are any kids in your community that might enjoy a game of football or a trip to the cinema.

- Banks give financial support to all kinds of businesses. Pick a bank that has an ethical mission statement.

- Help with a social action project. Volunteer at a local soup kitchen, homeless run, kids club, or graffiti clean up. Give up a Saturday afternoon and see what you can do.

- Read newspapers, learn about what is happening in your community, the country and around the world. The more you know about a situation, the more you can do to help.

- When you find a need, or a situation that isn't as good as it could be, commit to praying about it.

- Write letters to your MP. They are your representative, so if you want something to change, keep telling them until it changes.

- Go on a campaign. Join a rally to voice your protest about injustice.

- Vote! If you are able to vote, don't waste it!

- Boycott companies whose ethical motivation you don't agree with, such as clothing companies that use sweat shops or those that trade unjustly in the developing world.

Further reading

To get started ...

Rich Thinking About the World's Poor, Peter Meadows, Authentic Lifestyle, 2003

Ethical Shopping: Where To Shop, What to Buy and How To Make A Difference, William Young and Richard Welford, Fusion Press, 2002

Who Says You Can't Change the World?, Danny Smith, Authentic Lifestyle, 2003

Lift the Label, David Westlake and Esther Stansfield, Authentic Media, 2004

Trade Justice: A Christian Response to Global Poverty, Church House Publishing, 2004

The Street Children of Brazil, Sarah De Carvalho, Hodder & Stoughton Religious, 1996

In depth ...

Castrating Culture, Dewi Hughes, Paternoster Press, 2002

A Biblical View of Law and Justice, David McIlroy, Paternoster Press, 2004

Justice, Mercy and Humility, Tim Chester, Paternoster Press, 2002

Creating Space for Strangers, David Evans, InterVarsity Press, 2004

Bring me into the wide-open space where I'm vulnerable.
I'm a man now I have to move off the soluble.
Into daily encounters with God's living Spirit.
Take my hands off the wheel, close my eyes and let Him steer it.
To experiences and realms that I've never known.
Finish each day with a true sense that I've grown.
Faced my fears, prayed through the night.
Not to process information, but be given true sight.
Into the unknown, the untold, the unseen.
See the bigger picture that doesn't revolve around me.
Fall to my knees, surrender my abilities and use my availability
Standing on a stage, or when I'm in soliloquy.

MC McGLADIUS, 'vessels', from the album 'Full Time'
www.29thchapter.org.uk

outro

so you wanna be a history maker?

andy frost and jo wells

Have you ever bought a mobile phone? They always come with stacks of instructions for the 101 things that the phone can do. The instructions explain how to text message, how to go on the web, how to play games, how to take pictures and even how to make a phone call. But these instructions never teach mobile phone etiquette. The most puzzling question for me, is whether or not it is socially acceptable to answer the phone on the loo?

Jesus left the disciples and they were not quite sure what to do. They had no mission plan, no great strategy. They could have just locked themselves away from the world. Instead they waited upon the Holy Spirit and made history – the gospel spread like an epidemic.

What's next?

So you've read the book, you understand all the theory and maybe you have a few more practical ideas now. But what next? What do you do with all of this understanding?

We are not supposed to lock ourselves away with all our knowledge, away where it's safe and easy. We need to get out there. Live the life. All the ups, all the downs. Life with Jesus should cause an epidemic of history makers. Do you want to be one?

History maker

Is it true that when people pray
Cloudless skies will break
Kings and queens will shake
Yes it's true and I believe it
I'm living for you

Is it true that when people pray
We'll see dead men rise
And the blind set free
Yes it's true and I believe it
I'm living for you

I'm gonna be a history maker in this land
I'm gonna be a speaker of truth to all mankind
I'm gonna stand, I'm gonna run
Into your arms, into your arms again
Into your arms, into your arms again

Well it's true today that when people stand
With the fire of God, and the truth in hand
We'll see miracles, we'll see angels sing
We'll see broken hearts making history
Yes it's true and I believe it
We're living for you

History Maker, Martin Smith,
© 1996 Curious? Music UK

The Delirious song, 'History Maker', is one of my favourite tunes. It speaks of what happens when God uses us. It all kicks off with our relationship with Him. It begins as we run into His open arms. This song should become our prayer – that we will make history for Jesus.

Throughout the Bible, there are lists of people who have made history. Jabez is remembered as a man who prayed (1 Chr. 4:9–10). Enoch is remembered as a man who walked with God (Gen. 5:21–22). Rahab is remembered as a woman who was righteous (Jas. 2:25). When I die, I want to be known as someone who made history and saw lives transformed.

Maybe after reading this book, you are thinking, 'Yeah, I am up for this ...' but you fear that life will soon go back to normality. You will return to school, to college or back to work and you will start thinking, 'Man – this is too hard'. You will pray for change but it may seem like nothing happens. You will try reading your Bible and you might get bogged down. 'This is too hard, too demanding – impossible,' you think to yourself. Within the space of a week your passion has gone and you wait for the next spiritual high on the calendar.

The call to discipleship is about perseverance – pushing through the hard times.

The focus

Go for it! Take the risk. Jump in feet first. We're not promising that this is going to be easy. But we hope that when it gets tough, your relationship with Jesus will have sufficient foundations to carry you through.

A life with Jesus calls for discipline and faith. Work at keeping yourself on track. Every day is a new challenge and every day needs to be dedicated to God.

You are in your prime. I know you hear it all the time, and find it often hard to believe, but these really are the best years of your life. You will never be so mobile, so unattached, so free. Get out there. Don't die wishing 'If only ...' Know that even when you failed, you have at

least tried. Go for it freestyle – living in the freedom that
Christ offers and the style that He gives you.

So we ask the question again:
if not you, who? If not now, when?

Your thoughts?

So you've heard our thoughts on the key areas of discipleship but what do you think? What do you find hard?
What practical steps do you take to stay focused?

Check out www.sharejesusinternational.com/freestyle
to chat with others and share your suggestions.

Andy Frost and Jo Wells